THE NEW ICELANDERS
A North American Community

THE NEW ICELANDERS
A North American Community

Edited by
David Arnason & Vincent Arnason

TURNSTONE PRESS

Turnstone Press
607 – 100 Arthur Street
Winnipeg, Manitoba
Canada   R3B 1H3

Turnstone Press gratefully acknowledges the assistance of the Canada Council and the Manitoba Arts Council.

Unless otherwise stated, all photographs are from the Manitoba Archives. "The Smallpox Letter, March 13, 1877" and "Friðjón Friðricksson: Letters to Jón Bjarnason" are from the Manitoba Archives as well.

"Halfdan Sigmundsson, Mail Carrier" was previously published in *Brot af landnámssögu Nýja Íslands* (Columbia Press, 1923), translated by S. Stefanson in *Gimli Saga* (Gimli: Women's Institue, 1974). "Lord Dufferin's Visit," "A Few Hints to Icelandic Emigrants," "Journeys of Icelanders to America," "The Consitution of New Iceland" and "A Few Words About the Icelandic Settlement in Minnesota" were previously pubished in *Framfari*. "Jón Bjarnason" and "From the Secret Diary of Svanhildur Sigurdson, Age 12" were previously published in *Lögberg-Heimskringla*. "Thorgrímur Jónsson V" by Kristjana Gunnars was previously published in *Settlement Poems 2* (Turnstone Press, 1980). "Canada 1978" by W.D. Valgardson reprinted by permission from *The Carpenter of Dreams* (Skaldhús Press, 1986). "The Sunfish" by David Arnason was previously published in *Fifty Stories and a Piece of Advice* (Turnstone Press, 1982). "The Icelandic Emigration to Minneota, Minnesota" and "Vietnamese Cooking in Reykjavik" by Bill Holm reprinted by permission from *The Dead Get by With Everything* (Milkweed Press, 1990). "Have You Seen the Jólasveinar?" "Sources for the Icelandic Canadian Genealogist" and "Learning the Icelandic Language" were previously published in *The Icelandic Canadian*. Excerpts from "The Reminiscences of Simon Simonson," translated by William Kristjanson, were previously published in *The Icelandic Canadian*. "The Icelanders in Manitoba: The Myth of Beginnings" was previously published in *Border Crossings* magazine.

Front cover photograph: Robert Tinker
Back cover photograph from the collection of Kristin Kristofferson in the archives of Terry Tergesen.
Design: Manuela Dias

This book was printed and bound in Canada by Kromar Printing for Turnstone Press.
Second printing: May 1999

Canadian Cataloguing in Publication Data

The New Icelanders
ISBN 0-88801-186-5

1. Icelanders – Manitoba – History. 2. Icelanders – Minnesota – History. 3. Icelanders – North Dakota – History.
I. Arnason, David, 1940–   II. Arnason, Vincent, 1962–

FC3400.I3N4 1994   971.27'0043961   C94-920208-8
F1065.I2N4 1994

Contents

Preface

History is not just a record of what happened, where, and on what day. History is not out there somewhere, still happening, still accessible, weighted with truth. Instead, history is something we construct out of artifacts, memories, traces of a past that was once a present but is no more.

When we started to do the research for *The New Icelanders* we found the act of reconstruction was exciting. Out of letters, journals, documents, newspaper reports, interviews, photographs and artifacts, we found ourselves putting together a narrative, a story about a unique settlement in a new land, full of hope and despair, heroic deeds and bitter squabbles, in fact, all the things that make a human community.

But we found that the documents didn't always say the same thing. Eyewitnesses had completely different versions of the same story. The central figures of one narrative were bit players in anothers. The secondary sources, books and articles that purported to tell the true story disagreed with each other, and often were in direct disagreement with documents we found. And as we discussed the history of the Icelandic community and our own ancestors' parts in it, we found that even we were interpreting things in different ways, reading different narratives into the traces we found. It was clear that telling the truth about New Iceland was not going to be an easy task.

And so we decided to relinquish truth, and offer our readers two things: a set of documents that would let them construct their own narrative, and a number of different takes on the story by different people with a variety of experiences. If you want, you can read the constitution (and there are even conflicting translations), read the reports and newspapers and letters and accounts of the early settlers, and put together your own history. Or you can read the accounts of growing up Icelandic in Winnipeg or Minneota or Mountain or Gimli, and share in another writer's vision of what was. You can read poems and short stories that try to reinvent the vanished world. You can use the photographs to help you imagine the changing worlds of the settlers and their descendants. Or you can follow the recipes and cook your way back into a culture.

However you approach the book, we want you to think of yourself as a co-author, or perhaps as a co-conspirator in making history. We are daily offered the prospect of a new world of interactive computers and television and communications media. Think of this as an interactive book. Don't just read it. Make your own history.

David Arnason
Vincent Arnason

Sybil's Song

Now the land sinks beneath the sea.
The sun goes black.
Heaven is stripped of its bright stars.
The fires of the world ash rage,
throw steam and flames to heaven itself.

I read the future, the twilight of the doomed gods.

I see the green of growing things again.
The earth arises from the sea,
the eagle hunts for fish
in the torrent of waters.

Well, would you know more?

Óðinn will wield the blood wand of prophecy.
Baldur and Höður, the sons of his brothers
will set up their dwelling
in wide Wind-Home.

Well, would you know more?

I see a hall, fairer than sunlight
thatched with red gold.
That place is Gimli.
There the guiltless gods
will live in ease forever.

Freely translated by David Arnason from
Völuspá (The song of the Sybil) from *The Elder Edda*.

Fjallkonan

1

Sigtryggur Jonasson, father of the New Iceland colony.

The Icelanders in Manitoba: The Myth of Beginnings

The Icelandic community in North America has a peculiarly distinctive shape. Although it has been over a hundred years since the establishment of the first major settlement of Icelanders in North America, the community survives as a recognizable group. It has national and international organizations, a newspaper, *Lögberg-Heimskringla*, a magazine, *The Icelandic Canadian,* and a cohesiveness that allows members to feel themselves part of a group. This continues to be the case even among third and fourth generation Icelandic Canadians and Americans who do not speak the language and who have never been to Iceland.

Most ethnic groups struggle profoundly with the problem of maintaining identity, especially in the United States, where the melting pot program actively discourages ethnic allegiances. Even in Canada, the third generation of most ethnic groups has lost any sense of original identity. There are some very special reasons for the amazing durability of the North American Icelandic community and a festival called *Íslendingadagurinn* plays an important role in sustaining and nourishing the elusive goal of group identity.

The first permanent settlement of Icelanders in North America was established in Gimli, Manitoba, October 21, 1875 at 4:30 pm. On that day, the first day of winter according to the Icelandic calendar, 285 persons landed at Willow Island just south of the present site of Gimli, and by the evening of their arrival, the number had swelled to 286. Jón Jóhannsson, or Jón á Bölstað, the first child had been born in the new world, and the land had thus been claimed.

The Icelandic settlement in Manitoba was unique in a number of ways, and the experience of the settlers was quite radically different from that of other ethnic groups that immigrated to the Canadian prairies. It was, to begin with, an apocalyptic event. A series of volcanic eruptions in Iceland between 1873 and 1875 had left nearly 5,000 Icelanders homeless. There was neither the room nor the economic base in Iceland during a period of recession to absorb the displaced, and this, combined with an invitation from the then Governor-General, Lord Dufferin, led to a move to migrate to Canada. It is significant that the emigrants did not move primarily because of economic disadvantage, though certainly economic conditions were not good. Nor did they move in reaction to political or religious conditions at home. The group that left was heterogeneous. The poor and the wealthy alike, professionals, craftsmen, fishermen and farmers, all made the move together. The Icelandic settlement was a representative slice of Icelandic society, not a single level, and in this way it was different from any other large group of settlers to come to Canada. The historian Louis B. Hartz points out that fragment-cultures leave their enemies behind when they move to new places. Instead of confronting opposing forces, they undergo a rich internal development. The Icelanders brought with them all the arguments from home, and they continued them here.

The Icelandic settlers chose to move to the shores of Lake Winnipeg for a number of reasons. Many of them were fishermen, and the lake was teeming with fish. The rich Portage plain which was an alternative possibility was suffering a grasshopper infestation when the initial exploration party arrived and so did not seem inviting. The shores of Lake Winnipeg were heavily wooded, and for Icelanders whose own forests had completely disappeared, an inexhaustible supply of firewood and building materials seemed attractive. Finally, the government of Canada offered them a degree of independence which was quite striking, but dependent on their settling in the district of Keewatin, north of the boundary of the postage-stamp province of Manitoba.

The details of the settlement, known as the Icelandic Preserve or the Republic of New Iceland, depending on who refers to it, are quite unique. The Icelandic settlers were given an area about forty-two miles long and about eleven miles wide, stretching along the shores of Lake Winnipeg from Boundary Creek at the site of the present Winnipeg Beach to the Icelandic river and including Hecla Island. Only Icelanders were permitted to settle in this area. The Icelanders were guaranteed the use of Icelandic as their official language in perpetuity. English Criminal law was in effect, but the Icelanders were permitted to use their own civil law, which they did, writing a charter that was distinctly different from either English or Icelandic law. It had, for example, an elaborate system of social welfare and support for widows and the indigent. The franchise was extended to all gainfully employed men of good character over the age of eighteen. All men over the age of twenty-one years old, except for school teachers and ministers of the gospel were eligible for office.

The entire district was called *Vatnsþing,* or Lake Country. The republic was divided into four districts, *Víðirnesbyggð, Árnesbyggð, Fljótsbyggð* and *Miklejarbyggð.* The districts operated independently for the most part, but once a year on March 11, they met at Gimli to discuss large problems and changes to the constitution. The records were kept in five books. Book one contained the minutes of meetings. Book two contained census figures, book three, records of road building, book four, vital statistics including births, marriages and deaths, and book five, records of land transactions and land values. The details of the constitution are quite complex, but it was a remarkable document for its day.

The myth of beginnings is important to understanding the experience of the Icelandic community. Other prairie communities were named after people (MacGregor, McCreary) or old-country places (Balmoral, Sans Souci) or Indian place names (Winnipeg, Pinawa). Gimli, the site of the first settlement was named for the great Hall of Gimli in Norse mythology. The elder *Edda* tells us that after Ragnarök, when Fenrir kills Óðinn, and the wolves Skoll and Hati eat the sun and the moon, when Yggdrasill, the world ash, is shaken, and the gods are defeated in final battle, all the universe will return to fire and sea. Out of that will arise an island on which will be situated the Great Hall of Gimli. All the best of men, of giants, of gods and the creatures of outer darkness will be gathered here. (It's a tough place to get into: only a few gods will make it.) That post-apocalyptic vision is a perfect naming for people whose homes have literally disappeared under fire.

Let me tell you the story as it is told to children of the community. The Icelanders left their homes because erupting volcanoes drove them into the icy sea. They travelled for months in terrible hardship across the ocean. When they arrived in Canada, nothing was ready for them. They spent a year in Kinmount, Ontario before heading west. They crossed Lake Superior in a fierce storm, then made their way to St. Paul, Minnesota and travelled down the Red River. In Winnipeg, they hired three barges, enormous flatboats, which they dragged down the Red River until they reached the mouth. There, they were met by the Hudson's Bay Company steamer, the only steamer on Lake Winnipeg. They were on their way to the Icelandic River, but it was late in the year and a fall storm came up. The Captain cut the barges adrift and they floated in to shore. They landed by a giant white rock, the only large white rock on the south side of Lake Winnipeg, and the first Icelandic baby in the new world was born there in the shelter of the rock.

The first winter was the coldest winter in history, and the settlers had to live in tents given them by the Hudson's

Bay Company and rough log cabins which they built although it was so late in the season that the ground was frozen and they had trouble finding mud to chink the cracks. It was a difficult time for these settlers. They were unused to axes. Iceland had no trees. They didn't know how to fish under ice. In Iceland, the ocean didn't freeze.

The next summer there was a great smallpox epidemic, and one hundred and two people died. The epidemic lasted for over a year, and the community was tested by isolation and fear when it was quarantined. No one was allowed in or out. Families were separated and there was almost no help for the dying. Over the next twelve years, there were nine years of flood and a plague of locusts. It should have been the end, but it wasn't. The people named all the farms, more settlers came, and the community thrived.

My own memories of growing up are tied to that act of naming. I was born at *Espihóll,* a farm whose name echoes a famous farm from the *Njálssaga.* My grandfather farmed *Mýrar* and *Grœnamörk* as well. To the south of us was *Bólstaður* and to the north *Staraskógur.*

Most of this story told to children is factually true, but more important, it is also mythically true. Both metaphorically and literally cut adrift, the Icelanders make an accidental landing at the wrong place, which is nevertheless signalled to be the proper place by the miraculous white rock. They face a purification by disease, a testing by flood, a plague of locusts, an act of naming. They undergo the same process of claiming a country that is described in the old Icelandic *Landnámabók,* the book that describes the discovery of Iceland.

There is even more. A fierce religious dispute split the community in two. The Reverend Páll Thorláksson and the reverend Jón Bjarnason led the opposing factions, the *Pálls Menn* and the *Jóns Menn.* Páll Thorláksson represented the stricter Evangelical Icelandic Lutheran group, associated with the American Norwegian Synod, while Jón Bjarnason led the more liberal Icelandic Lutherans, many of whom

c. 1920, Hecla Island (Mikley).

Thorgrímur Jónsson V

burn out the old year
at grund, jóhann briem's
place, new year's eve
1876, those able

to walk are out

what's left of my
eyes protrudes (can't
fish this winter
smallpox overlaps

into hunting, building)
i'm the hunted now

live under dead
leaves, my people

without time left
to construct (keep going

on government loans)
maybe next year, spring
leaves will stir, fish
burst out

of dead ice, dead
flakes on the ground
maybe what's left

of my people will walk
away from this place

maybe next year

—Kristjana Gunnars

5

c. 1885. Johannes Sveinsson Holm and Soffia Vilhjálmsdottir,
great grandparents of Bill Holm.
Photo courtesy Bill Holm.

later became Unitarians. Páll did not like the Gimli settlement. He admired the American system and mistrusted the British. He felt that Icelanders would do better to assimilate in the United States than they would in their own settlement in Canada. He led his followers to Argyle, and from there to Saskatchewan and North Dakota. An Icelandic diaspora in the new world had begun.

Like any other group, the Icelanders came to Canada to settle. The numbers, the dates, the place names, the maps are all available to the historian. But the facts are not the story. My point is that geography is not an unmediated presence, a set of simple, undeniable truths about the world. Any understanding of a landscape is an understanding mediated by culture and experience.

So the Icelanders who moved to Manitoba played out a version of the founding of Iceland in their founding of New Iceland. They settled on Lake Winnipeg. It would be easy to argue that Icelanders are fishermen, and so they chose to live on a lake. But they were not lake fishermen. They had to learn to fish all over again, setting nets instead of trolling them, fishing at least for part of the time through four feet of ice. They were taught to fish by the Indians, and they developed a very special relationship with the Indians through that experience.

The floods that wiped out their work again and again were accepted as necessary and inescapable, a new testing. The more practical Ukrainians who came after 1897 immediately dismantled the beaver dams on the ridge west of the settlement which were the cause of the flooding, and put an end to it.

The truth of some of my details might be disputed. Perhaps things did not happen in just such a way. In fact, the Icelanders were probably not cut adrift and left to land in the storm. More likely, they were hauled through the channel to the quiet waters of the lagoon behind Willow Point. But I'm not interested in some narrow historic truth here. I'm more interested in a good, serviceable mythic truth.

The Republic of New Iceland lasted for twelve years, from 1875 to 1887. It was incorporated into an expanded Manitoba in 1881, but it didn't lose all its special rights immediately. It maintained its system of government until 1887. Only Icelanders were allowed into the area until 1897, when it was finally opened to other settlers. The new settlers turned out to be mostly Ukrainian and Polish, peasants with a feel for farming. The Icelandic settlement turned out to be basically urban. There was no equivalent in Iceland for the large isolated farm, and when the Ukrainian farmers arrived, many of the Icelanders breathed a sigh of relief, sold off their homesteads and moved into

1921, S.S. "Lady of the Lake" in Gimli harbour.

towns and cities. They largely abandoned the countryside to the Ukrainians. This turned out to be a workable system. The Ukrainians who came were a socially uniform group. They were only farmers. The Icelanders became the group of merchants who served the new community.

The Icelandic community is one of the oldest ethnic communities on the prairies. Only the Mennonites who arrived at about the same time have as long a history. And yet, in spite of the fact that the communities have largely dispersed, that the old settlements like Gimli and Riverton and Arborg are no longer even largely Icelandic, there continues to exist a large and vital Icelandic presence on the prairies. The Icelanders continue to publish a newspaper. They have several active cultural institutions such as the Icelandic Frón and the Icelandic National League. Where later immigrants to Manitoba such as the Norwegians, the Swedes and the Germans have largely been so integrated that there is little sign of their cultural presence, the Icelanders continue to form a significant cultural group. The source of this cohesiveness is the the myth of beginnings, a myth shared by Icelandic-Canadians and Icelandic-Americans as well. We look backward, not to some lost haven across the sea in Iceland, but to our roots as a people in a new land. When we hold our celebrations, we honour the old country but we celebrate the new as well. When we tell our epic stories, they are stories located in the new land, stories like the horrors of the Smallpox Epidemic, when the bodies of children were stacked on the roofs of houses so that wolves would not get at them until they could be buried in the spring. Or even lighter stories, like the marriage of Caroline Taylor and Sigurður Kristófersson, which took place on Netley Creek, the happy couple on one side and the Métis minister in a boat in the middle of the creek shouting out the ceremony. We even have our own anthem, Guttormur Guttormsson's poem *Sandy Bar,* a powerful evocation of the sadness of the pioneer experience, and a poem more important to Icelanders in North America than any of the great Icelandic medieval epics.

And finally, we have our own carnival, our special celebration, *Íslendingadagurinn*. For many years, it has been the central event of the Icelandic experience in North America. Firmly located in time and space: Gimli, the first Monday of August, it is the focal point of our thinking of ourselves as a group. Here, we are ruled by our *Fjallkona,* the maid of the mountain, not some young girl celebrated solely for her physical beauty, but an older woman, earth mother, celebrated for her contribution to the community as a whole. It is a wonderful and entirely unique position, a creation of the community here and not an imported ceremony from Iceland. (The *Fjallkona* had been a somewhat different figure in earlier ceremonies in Iceland, though the role had pretty much disappeared there. Her success in the new world revitalized her as a figure in Iceland.)

At *Íslendingadagurinn,* we gather from all over the continent, we renew acquaintants, we hold family reunions and, most importantly, we renew the myth of our beginnings, and in that myth we find a sense of community that holds together a dispersed people who have entered thoroughly into the national mythologies of Canada and the United States. Because of the hold of that myth, it is possible to think of yourself a a New Icelander even if you speak no Icelandic and have never been to Iceland

Even more importantly, the myth of beginnings ties together the Icelandic community of North America with the other communities of Manitoba which help us celebrate. For the Ukrainians the Poles, the British, the Germans and all the other races and groups that make up the community of the Interlake, the founding myth is also their story, *Íslendingadagurinn* also their celebration. As contemporary North Americans we live in many cultures at the same time. We wish to protect our own, but also to share it. *Íslendingadagurinn* and the myth of beginnings it celebrates is important to Canada. It gives us one more valid way of being Canadian without evoking ancient dreams of Empire.

Þorgeir's Bull, Painting by Michael Olito

Þorgeir's Bull is a painting based on an old Icelandic folk tale. The story goes that in the early eighteen hundreds a farmer in Iceland had killed his bull and was in the process of skinning it when his wife called him in for supper. When he returned, the bull had miraculously come to life and was running away across a field, dragging his skin behind him. The bull vowed to haunt Þorgeir's family for nine generations.

In 1875, Þorgeir's family was among the settlers who came to New Iceland in Manitoba. They settled in the area around Arborg. Þorgeir's bull, of course, came with them, and now resides in Manitoba. Sometimes he can be seen in the distance, running across a field. Most often he comes as a barking dog at night.

Olito's painting depicts the rebirth of a European myth in the new world. The bull is stepping out of his old European bones and entering the new world. He has forsaken the mountains of Iceland for the plains of Manitoba. The ghost is powerful, and the violent colours are in keeping with the intent of the painting. Transplanting ghosts and myths is a violent undertaking.

Photo courtesy Michael Olito.

c. 1875, Friðjón Friðricksson.

Friðjón Friðricksson: Letters to Jón Bjarnason

TORONTO, NOVEMBER 14, 1874

Most honorable friend:

I thank you very much for your letter which I received yesterday (it had been at the P.O. for four days). I was really glad to get your letter and to learn that you are well. I also appreciated your interest in our countrymen who have moved to this country. I only wish that we had more patriots, like yourself, among us, but unfortunately that is not the case, at all.

You asked me to tell you about Icelanders in Canada, and I shall do my best to do so: Last August 111 people moved from Iceland to Ontario, and in addition to these 14 more arrived, i.e. 125 in all. Of these (125) 23 people have moved to the states, but six have passed away, maybe more. According to this reckoning 96 – out of those who came last year – are here. In addition to this group one person has been here since the summer of 1872. In August of last year, a man with his wife and four children came here from the southern part of Iceland. The majority of these 103 Icelanders stay in Muskoka in Parry Sound, Rosseau and surroundings, and a few live here in Toronto. Only two or three farmers have broken land and built houses for themselves, but I don't know how successful their farming is. All others work as hired hands, some in saw mills, some in factories or have other odd jobs; most are farm hands. The Icelanders who came here in September of last year are 352, most of these came from the counties of: Skagafjörður, Eyjafjörður, Þingeyjar.

The State Government of Ontario asked Sigtryggur Jónasson from Skjaldarvik in Eyjafjörður County (he has been here for two years) to meet these Icelanders at Quebec. He accompanied them to Toronto. A few bachelors were immediately engaged in digging ditches in the country and maids (or women servants) were assisted in finding jobs, but the majority of this group stayed for two weeks in the Emmigrant House. Then they were transferred to a small town, Kinmount, which is 120 miles northeast of here. Houses are being built in Kinmount in which the Icelanders will live during the winter. The Government is going to provide Icelanders with land in the vicinity of Kinmount and to give them steady jobs with the railroad. This railroad is to connect Lake Ontario to the Pacific Line, crossing the district where the Icelanders are supposed to live.

There are very few stores north there making it difficult to get food and other necessities. In order to improve this situation, Sigtryggur Jónasson (along with a Canadian) established a business there – selling to the Icelanders everything that they need. I had correspondence with a fellow north there, bringing me a lot of unpleasant news: At first housing was insufficient, the people became ill with stomach problems and other illnesses, and 20 died – mostly children and teenagers. The reason why this illness struck is probably poor housing and dismal sanitary conditions – phenomena which have tended to be associated with the Icelanders. Now the health situation is improving. The land up north seems to be barren, but only a small part of it has been explored. Many are discontent; they think that the Government is failing to fulfill its promises about high salaries and good housing, but these accusations are mostly due to foolishness and avarice since the Government tries to do its best to make their (Icelanders) lives tolerable.

The Icelanders complain about not having a minister, and have a good reason to. It is absolutely awful that children's education is totally neglected. Recently I got a letter from Sigtryggur Jónasson concerning this matter. I hereby send it to you and ask you to give us some indication as to whether or not you would be willing to take this job. I know that this job will be more difficult than the average one in Iceland but, on the other hand, the need is so acute that it is hard to have to turn the job down. However, I advise you not to rush into this, at least not until we can be sure that Icelanders settle down here and form a community.

Concerning an "Icelandic Association" I shall do my best, but it is difficult to discuss the matter with the Icelanders because most of them live far away from me – out in the country. I am going to appoint several local agents to assist me in promoting the matter. However, I am not very optimistic about this association except maybe if we were to divide it into two bodies, each with its own board of directors, one of which would be located where the majority of the Icelanders live. While the board of directors is located in the States, Icelanders in Canada cannot attend meetings and therefore it is difficult for us to join. When I have brought this matter up to the Icelanders, I shall write to you and tell you about the results. Anyway I hope to be able to provide the list of names.

I and my wife are well. I have a neat (clean) and rather easy job in a shoe repair shop. It doesn't pay much, but I can manage, and I like it much better than in Milwaukee.

Pardon my rush in writing this letter which I send to you with best wishes for you and your wife.

Yours,

Friðjón Friðricksson

KINMOUNT, JUNE 15, 1875

Dear Friend:

. . . Early last winter Icelanders here started to become discontented. They found the work at the railroad hard, they found the salaries low (a dollar a day) and there were many more grievances, some reasonable, but others were pure imagination as a result of deadly false ideas about America which Icelanders both here and in Iceland possess. For instance, they think that every puddle here is full of various kinds of fish and all they have to do is to choose which fish to grab for their next meal. They think that the forests are full of birds and wild animals which can be caught whenever one needs food. Furthermore, they expect to be able to keep their jobs even if they only show up for work two or three days a week. When these hopes turned out to be illusions, many Icelanders became desperate. They thought that the Government of Ontario had brought them to a miserable place, and they wanted to get away. One day Jóhannes Arngrímsson, who you know from Milwaukee, joined the Icelanders. He was supposed to be an interpreter for the Icelanders and he was paid by the railroad company. He took the opportunity to turn Icelanders against the Government of Ontario and to direct their thoughts toward Nova Scotia because the Government there was interested in getting Icelanders to Nova Scotia. Icelanders now became so overly excited that they took up money collection in order to finance a trip for Jóhannes to Halifax. He left, along with three or four others, for Halifax for the purposes of asking the Government to finance the transfer of Icelanders from Ontario to Nova Scotia. This request was turned down, naturally, because it is most unbecoming for union states to compete with one another this way. Then Jóhannes and his companions started to write praises about Nova Scotia to their followers, most of which had no foundation in reality but revealed utter stupidity and hostility towards those who opposed his plan.

On March the fifteenth, the work at the railroad was

discontinued and the Icelanders consequently lost their jobs and started to move away, but instead of looking for jobs in other places throughout the state they sat idle in Lindsey and waited for new special laws – concerning Icelandic emmigrants moving to Nova Scotia – to be passed.

Finally in May those – 42 in all – who were the best off financially, spent their last cent to move to Nova Scotia. According to reports, they have been well received; they have either been given money or they have been able to borrow money in order to sustain themselves for the time being. They have been promised land, 30 miles from the shore, and they have been promised work in road building in the vicinity. Incidentally, because their letters include such an overwhelming amount of nonsense, it is difficult to know what is true in their writing. Jóhannes is now in Iceland to try to get Icelanders to move to Nova Scotia. Those here have started to lose interest in Nova Scotia for the time being but they wonder how things are going to turn out.

There are still approximately 160 Icelanders in Kinmount. Of these, two farmers have bought land and three have leased land for one year. Many others have started to grow potatoes in various places and therefore consider themselves settled, at least until next fall.

Our main problem here is unemployment; there are no jobs available in the vicinity. Throughout the spring we were hoping for the railroad work to begin, but all in vain, because the railroad company has financial problems. The Government is not responding to the company's request for assistance because there are so many other railroads under construction and the various companies are all asking for "bonuses" from the Government. However, most hope that the railroad to Kinmount will be built next fall – bringing an enormous prosperity to our district.

More than 20 Icelanders accepted " 'Free-Grant' land" this spring – most of it four to ten miles from Kinmount. They say it is good land, covered with forest, but because of poverty they have no means of working it this summer. Therefore, they are bound to seek jobs far away – if the railroad construction does not begin in the immediate future. Some have already gone, leaving their families behind. In general terms, lack of employment and depression is worse than usual throughout the state of Ontario – and salaries are extremely low . . .

. . . We here in Kinmount, like many other Icelanders, are hoping very strongly for the establishment of a united Icelandic colony. However, even though this seems to be fairly suitable for such a colony, we realize that it would not be satisfactory because the land available is not large enough for us to be able to be separated from the original inhabitants, forcing us to mingle with these aboriginals to such a degree that it would be impossible for us to preserve those traits of our own culture which are worthwhile keeping: Our language and our religion.

Some time ago we had a meeting where we discussed this matter and we reached the conclusion that the best thing to do for the time being was to send some representatives to the State of Manitoba because there are a lot of possibilities in that State not to be found elsewhere. There is, for instance, spacious land very suitable for farming (both for growing corn, etc. and for animal farming) and hopefully the Government is willing to provide Icelanders with some of this land. We selected two Icelanders for this mission, Sigtryggur Jónasson and Einar Jónasson (who is from the western part of Iceland) and an old gentleman by the name of John Taylor is going to join them. We also sent the Government of the Union States an appeal to finance the journey (for these three men) and we are hopeful that this request will be granted. If the land turns out to be good, one more colony for Icelanders will be available in addition to those which until now have been in the making . . .

Manitoba Free Press, 1875

JULY 17, 1875

Icelanders

Rev. Mr. Taylor, Moravian missionary, formerly of Iceland and five Icelanders, are now here. These gentlemen comprise a deputation from their countrymen, to examine this Province with a view to the settlement of the whole of their people here, they being dissatisfied with Ontario and the United States. Their principal requirements being fishing and hunting, we would suggest the neighbourhood of Manitoba and Winnipegooses Lakes. Some one ought to take them in hand, and show them the country.

JULY 20, 1875

The Icelandic Deputation

To the Editor of the Free Press.

I regret to learn that the Iceland delegation has been allowed to leave for Lake Winnipeg to view the country for settlement alone. Our neighbours know how to do these things better. Here is an immigration of 30,000 people going begging and this flourishing Province and City cannot afford even courting the delegation. They should have been shown the country around Lake Manitoba and Winnipeg in ordinary comfort and under intelligent guidance. If our economical City and Provincial Governments have no finances for such purposes a subscription could have been raised from citizens.

July 20th, 1875
Senex.

[Editor's Remarks. – In reference to the above, our correspondent is perhaps unaware of all the circumstances attending the visit of the delegation mentioned. The deputation started this morning in a Hudson's Bay York boat; which has been placed at their disposal by the Hudson's Bay Company. Col. Smith also kindly supplied them with tents. And Mr Codd, Dom. Lands Agent, here gave them a letter to Mr. Vaugham, DLS, than whom few men are better acquainted with the section of country they intend prospecting, asking him to render them all assistance possible. His Honor the Lieut-Governor has interested himself very much in the welfare of the delegation; and they feel well pleased at the attention they are now receiving. However, we think the Dominion Government, did not give them credentials to the officers here that they should. What has been done is local effort entirely. We think the Dominion Government should have taken them in tow in the same manner that they did the Mennonites.]

AUGUST 4, 1875.

The Icelandic Delegation

To the Editor of the Free Press.

Sir: Permit me through the columns of the Free Press to make a few remarks on the occasion of my leaving Manitoba to return to Ontario.

Having been enabled through the enlightened and vigorous policy of the Administration at Ottawa to visit this country with a deputation of Icelanders, for the purpose of seeking some suitable locality for the establishment of a colony from Iceland, I have the pleasure of being able to say that I have met with a hearty welcome from almost every quarter, and that in consequence, my labors have been much facilitated, and a result as favorable as we could reasonably expect more easily arrived at.

Our choice of a reserve has been made in a direction where it is least likely to interfere with anyone, that is, on the western shore of Lake Winnipeg. It seems remarkably well adapted for the Icelanders. The two great natural provisions of fish and pasturage are found there abundantly. The long and severe winter will not probably far exceed that to which they are accustomed. Whilst the rich lands will produce crops of grain not much inferior to those of Manitoba in general. The place is easy of access by water, and a good winter road is to be found on the ice. Altogether we can see no reason why there should not be a prosperous thriving settlement fully established there in a short time. The first emigration from Iceland would probably reach Fort Garry in May. Some 40 or 50 families, now in Ontario, would come here this fall in time for fishing, if the necessary arrangements can be made for them to settle here. Three men of the party now here will remain until these arrangements are carried out. They have gone down to the railway crossing at present.

We desire to acknowledge the kind consideration which we have met with from the Governor of Manitoba and from many friends in Winnipeg. Our thanks are tendered to the Mayor for his uniform politeness and readiness to oblige us in every way. To him and to Messrs. Sinclair, Luxton, and Wright, we owe the pleasure of a ride over the prairies on the Assiniboine to visit the farms where the plague of grasshoppers had not destroyed the crops. We have great reason to remember the kind assistance obtained from Mr. McTavish, of the HB Co., by which we were enabled to visit the Lake in much comfort and safety. Also, Mr. Flett, of the Lower Fort, who kindly helped and entertained us on the way. To Mr. Nixon we are indebted for the loan of tents and coverings for the men. The services of our trusty guide, Monkman, were really indispensable, and our quick and successful trip is due to him.

Finally, we would make special mention of the polite assistance afforded us by the gentlemen of the Dominion Lands Office, and by Donald Codd, Esq., in particular. If we are to regard this gentleman as an index of the disposition of the Government towards our proposed settlement, we have indeed much cause for self congratulation.

Trusting that the Lord will so graciously overrule and direct the future progress of this work as He has already led us and prospered us hitherto,

I remain, etc.

John Taylor,

On behalf of the Icelandic Deputation.

John Taylor, Canadian agent for the New Iceland Colony.

AUGUST 11, 1875

John Taylor's Exploration Journal

According to promise we are enabled to lay before our readers a few particulars of the proceedings of the Icelandic deputation which have, for the most part, recently departed from this place on their return to Ontario, whence they were sent forth on their work of exploration. After conferring with our agent of Crown Lands, Donald Codd Esq., it was finally arranged that the first visit should be made to that locality which seemed most likely to meet the requirements of the people, namely the western coast of Lake Winnipeg. Accordingly, aided by the very kind arrangements made for them by Mr. McTavish who furnished them with one of the large Hudson's Bay Company boats free of all charge, and provided them with camp necessaries of every description needed for the trip, on the most liberal terms, the party left Fort Garry on Tuesday evening 20th of July last and reached the Stone Fort the same night. The H.B. Co. officer in charge, Mr. Flett, of whose kindness and hospitality, grateful mention is made, furnished them with mast, rigging, sail, tarpaulin, tow-line and many other things needed to render their outfit complete. On Wednesday they were only able to proceed 12 or 15 miles further and a strong north wind kept them in camp all the next day. Much information was obtained at Selkirk from Mr. Vaughan and his sons, who had surveyed the coast and who showed much interest in this exploration. On Friday morning 23rd while taking a hurried meal at 4 a.m. the party was joined by Monkman, the best guide they could possibly have had with them, and who we are glad to learn, fully sustained his high reputation during the trip. Dr. Schultz accompanied Monkman to the boat but did not proceed with the party. Two Half-breeds were already engaged with the boat from Fort Garry, one of whom acted as the steersman and the other as cook and bowman. By rowing and sailing the mouth of the river was reached by 9 a.m. It was with surprise and delight that they looked around them on the great sea of waving grass ready for the scythe or the mowing machine, and extending to parts unknown, the great inexhaustible supply of winter feed for flocks and herds in years to come, and before them lay the waters of the great Lake Winnipeg, asleep and quiet.

"All the rush and the roar of the angry waters" (we are quoting now from Mr. Taylor's notes made during his tour) "lashed into fury with three days' north wind had quite subsided. It was with a sense of regained freedom we looked out on the noble expanse of water, extending so very far northward to Norway House and the Saskatchewan River. From Moorhead we had traced the Red River for 700 miles through its many windings, growing insensibly larger until we now stood at its mouth where in several wide channels it pours its waters into this great basin. As we round on to the western shore of the lake we perceived a schooner under sail for Fort Alexander on the south-east corner of the lake, and two large boats like our own coming out of the river by a more easterly channel than the one we had used. In this wonderful land of progress, who can tell how soon this river mouth may be bustling with the many masts of lake-going vessels, laden with rich products from the far off plains of the mighty Saskatchewan and other parts. Shall the trading craft of our Icelanders be among them? Who knows? Having got well to windward under shelter of the land, we sailed along with a west wind, close enough to shore to enable us to verify the statements of our guide. A white sandy beach without a rock to be seen marked the shore nearly all the way to Willow Island, 15 miles from the mouth of Red River. A few houses were nearby where two young Englishmen were establishing themselves on good farms. As we proposed indulging ourselves in a visit to them on our way back, we did not stop but kept on with a pleasant little breeze to Willow Island. Here we beached our boat and took our skiff on board as the wind was freshening. We had before tried to obtain stones for ballast, but succeeded only in raising a few boulders out of the water which covered the reef. Leaving Willow Island at 1:30 p.m. we stood northward and in three hours were up to Drunken River 18 miles further, a long stretch from one shelter to another. But the wind was favourable now, though a change was at hand so we resolved on carrying our original intention of camping on Sandy Bar 12 or 15 miles further. Our Half-breed boatmen were very unwilling to go so far north, but as they had both fallen asleep over their pipes, and Monkman was at the helm, we stood on our course, and were 6 or 8 miles north of Drunken River when they awoke. It was very hard to repress our laughter when the men awoke, scratching their heads and looking to windward with a perplexed and bewildered gaze, at last compre-hended the situation by perceiving Big Island only a few miles ahead of us.

The wind failing we took again to the oars, and at 7:30 beached the boat on Sandy Bar a long spit of sand which extends one or two miles out from the main land towards Big Island. As the sky was cloudy and threatening, our tents were quickly set up, and in less than an hour the wind came tearing down upon us from the north. Had we not landed so soon we must have been driven back or swamped by it. As it is we are sheltered by the narrow Sandy Bar and the wide bay to the north of us. The mosquitos were unusually bad when we first stepped ashore, but as soon as ever the north wind struck us, there was not a solitary one moving. The two boats that had left Red River with us in the morning had kept company during the day but had passed us in the evening and had gone into the large harbour for the night. They are traders bound for Saskatchewan. Indian huts are pitched near us and their wolfish looking dogs are searching everything as if they were regular customs officers. Saturday morning came with unsettled weather. After breakfasting on Winnipeg fish, of which it required a prodigious quantity to satisfy our party of ten (a fact which speaks well either for the appetites of the men or for the good quality of the fish just taken out of the nets), we resumed our journey, which we were now able to do in spite of the strong opposition of the north

wind, because of the shelter of the fine bay into which we tracked or hauled the boat. If this is to become our settlement, we propose naming it after the youngest of our party, Brisjau harbor. It is five miles long and three to four miles wide, well protected on all sides, and having a good channel at each end for entry or departure. It will be a notable place when the country becomes settled.

Sailing across the harbour we found sufficient shelter within banks of rushes to permit us rowing to the mouth of the river which we propose exploring for our first settlement. It is of ample width near the mouth and for several miles up we found 7 feet water, and one fourth of a mile across. The wide fields of rushes, and of grass that we found at the mouth of Red River were repeated here

1935, Pounding storm on Lake Winnipeg at Gimli Harbour.

only on a smaller scale. We had set our minds upon this place before leaving Fort Garry, and few can understand the deep interest we felt as we proceeded up. After passing the extensive hay marshes we came to higher banks with poplars about 4 miles from the mouth. The land became higher as we proceeded until the banks were 20 feet above the river. At about 8 miles up the river narrowed to half or two chains, and an Indian dam was thrown across the stream for fishing purposes, the water being shoal. Finding our further progress stopped we camped and sent out parties to gather further information. As our guides knew nothing of these parts, and finding that the shallow rapids extended some long distance, we postponed further operations until Monday. The country was exactly what we wanted as far as we had now come, and our first Sabbath service was fervent and solemn. After our closing hymn

(O God of Bethel) had been sung, Monkman gave free expression to his emotion, "A settlement thus began," he said, "cannot fail to be a blessing to this country. Every Indian for miles round would have gladly been here today, had they known we were to have religious services." May the precious recollection of this solemn service in the far off North-West never be forgotten by any of us. And if the lord shall plant the colony of Icelanders here, may there never be wanting among them true and devoted hearts to serve the living God. Home and loved ones were not forgotten before the throne of the heavenly grace. Many a fervent petition we know is ascending this day in our behalf for the blessing to our work, from the loving hearts of brethren in Ontario.

Our work of exploration was vigorously followed up by two parties into which we had divided ourselves. The

1907, Dog teams going from Gimli to Norway House.

18

skiff was hauled through the rapids for four miles by one party who waded through, until the river again became fit for boating and 8 to 10 miles of progress from camp satisfied them that the country improved at every step. Hay marshes were more frequent and extensive, and the land, as far as it was examined on both sides of the river, was of the best quality, the timber being more mixed and large spruce and poplar more frequent. The second party were equally well rewarded, and a fine site for our first settlement was met with, to which vessels drawing 6 or 7 feet of water very easily approach. Our reunited party camped for the night at a rich expanse of waving grass, just fit for the haymaker. What a heavy crop to the acre, and what a wonderful stretch of country thus richly covered seems perfectly bewildering. Our guns had procured for us both ducks and fish, which were greatly relished. The next party struck out from the river through the woods, and the result of all further examination proved to our entire satisfaction that this was the very place where an Icelandic settlement might be made with every reasonable prospect of success. Returning we came upon a party of Indians just arrived from Norway House and purposing to settle near here. They seemed uncertain about the place until the treaty with the Governor had been made. Our last lake camp was on a sandy beach. A storm from south-west made very rough and many grasshoppers fell from their elevated flights. The shores were blackened by their numbers. These seemed to have been arrested in their southernly flight by the gale and precipitated to the earth and the Lake. A severe thunder storm broke upon us and the rain fell in torrents. We placed rollers under our boat and drew her up beyond the reach of the surf, which dashed nearly to our tent door.

A north wind sprang up next morning and we started at 6 a.m. to look at the country to the south. But the wind soon increased and the heavy swell on the lake made it advisable to avoid landing. In six hours we had run 50 miles, through a heavy sea and amidst a long line of foam and breakers we re-entered the mouth of the Red River, thankful for its shelter and its smooth water. Driven southward by the freshing gale we reached Stone Fort and next day reached here (Fort Garry) again, having made the trip and accomplished our purpose in the unexpectedly and, I believe, unprecedently short period of 10 days.

Our reasons for selecting this lake country are, briefly as follows:
1. Absence of grasshoppers hitherto, and improbability of their ever coming there.
2. Good and easy access to the very spot – railway and steamboat every step of the journey from Quebec.
3. Excellent and abundant fishing.
4. Extensive hay marshes everywhere scattered through the entire region.
5. Superior quality of land. Deep black soil resting on a white clay.
6. Abundance of timber for building, fencing, fuel and for commercial purposes.
7. An extensive and well protected harbour.
8. Facilities of intercourse with Fort Garry and the Red and Assiniboine and other rivers both north and south.

The Canadian Pacific Railway is located to the west of our reserve. If any advantages are to be derived from this fact, and we trust they are not few, we have not based our selection entirely on them. Although the Icelanders are not regular navvies their experience has made them familiar with railway work to such an extent that no contractor on the extensive line can be otherwise than deeply interested in our proposed settlement. They have earned a good name where they have been at work, and a quiet, orderly and peaceable gang of burly Icelanders would be worthy of the enquiries of all connected with the construction of the line. As settlers in the country they would be in the development of it, and would be more reliable than most outsiders.

John Taylor

Monument to New Iceland settlers,
erected at Gimli, July 1938.

The Constitution of New Iceland

CHAPTER I.

THE SUB-DIVISION OF NEW ICELAND.

The Icelandic settlement at New Iceland is designated Vatnsþing i.e. The Lake District. (The word thing is used here in the sense of a political sub-division of a district or country. Translators note.) It shall be sub-divided into four districts, named Willow Point district, comprising townships 18 and 19, ranges 3 and 4 east; Arnes district, comprising townships 20 and 21, ranges 3 and 4 east; the River Settlement, comprising townships 22 and 23, ranges 3 and 4 east; and Big Island district, comprising all of Big Island.

CHAPTER II.

ELECTION OF DISTRICT COMMITTEES AND UMPIRES.

At an annual general meeting to be held on the 7th day of January, or on the 8th day when the 7th falls on a Sunday, the residents of each district shall elect five men to a committee to be known as the district committee, two umpires and one vice-umpire. Those committeemen who receive the greatest number of votes shall be considered to be duly elected, provided only that more than half of the residents of the district with voting privileges according to Chapter III are present. Should anyone decline to accept election at the meeting, others shall be chosen in their place, but should any of the committeemen die after having been elected, they shall be replaced by those who received the next highest number of votes after the men elected to the committee. Should the election of the fifth committeeman result in a tie, a decisive election must be held. The same regulations apply to the election of umpires as are set forth here for the election of committeemen.

CHAPTER III.

VOTING RIGHTS AND ELIGIBILITY TO HOLD OFFICE.

Every male 18 years of age who resides in, owns property in, is the head of a household or has permanent employment in a district, and has an unblemished reputation shall have the right to vote in elections of the district committee and umpires. All those with voting rights shall be eligible for election to the district committee, with the exception of clergymen serving the community and permanantly employed public school teachers. No one, however, shall be eligible for election who has not reached the age of 21 years.

CHAPTER IV.

RESPONSIBILITIES OF THE GENERAL PUBLIC.

Paragraph 1. Attendance at meetings. The residents of each district shall attend a general meeting to be held between March 15th and April 15th at the place and time determined by the reeves to discuss matters pertaining to the general welfare of the district.

Paragraph 2. Road work and road tax. Each male 21 years of age shall be responsible for putting in two days of work, 10 hours each day, annually on the construction of public roads, or shall pay the sum of two dollars into the funds for road construction of the district in which he resides. Those who have no permanent residence shall contribute their labour or money to the district in which they are residing when such work is under taken. Road construction shall proceed at the place and time determined by the district committees.

Paragraph 3. Reporting of deaths, births and marriages. The head of each household shall be responsible for reporting to his reeve the deaths and births occurring in his home within a week from the time they take place.

KLEINUR

Kleinur are ordinary cake doughnuts.

To make: Mix 1 cup sugar, 3 eggs, 2 tablespoons melted butter and 1 cup light cream. In another bowl, mix 4½ cups flour, 2 teaspoons baking powder and a pinch of salt. Make a hollow in dry ingredients and add wet. Roll out dough on a floured board. Deep fry. A typical Icelandic form is to cut dough into rectangles or diamonds 2 inches by 3 inches, cut a lengthwise slit, and pull one end through the slit to form a knot before frying.

Furthermore, every man who contracts marriage is responsible for reporting it to his reeve within the same space of time.

Paragraph 4. Statistical reports and census records. The residents and heads of households of each district shall be responsible for furnishing their reeve with a detailed report, annually before the end of the month of December, covering all aspects of their household economy as well as the number of individuals in their home. These reports shall be made on the forms provided for that purpose.

Paragraph 5. Support of widows and orphans. The residents of each district shall be responsible for supporting widows and orphans in accordance with regulations adopted by a majority of the residents of the district; they shall also assist those who for special reasons are unable to support themselves.

Paragraph 6. Building meetinghouses. The residents of each district shall provide themselves with a meetinghouse in the manner and at the location the majority deems most desirable.

Paragraph 7. Tax for general necessities. Every resident of each district who enjoys voting privileges shall pay annually the sum of 25 cents into the treasury of the district in which he resides, this money to be collected in a manner determined by the reeve. This tax shall be paid before the end of September each year.

CHAPTER V.
ELECTION OF REEVES, TREASURERS AND SECRETARIES.

Each district committee shall choose from among its own members a chairman, to be known as the reeve and also a vice-reeve. Vice-reeves shall assume the duties of

An early farmstead of log buildings with grass roofs.

the reeves in the event the latter are hindered from performing them. Each committee shall also choose from among its members a treasurer and secretary.

CHAPTER VI.
RESPONSIBILITIES OF THE DISTRICT COMMITTEES.

Paragraph 1. Maintenance of roads. The district committees shall be responsible for the construction and maintenance of roads in their respective districts.

Paragraph 2. Appointment of trustees and guardians. The committees shall assume responsibility for making sure widows have competent trustees and orphans trustworthy guardians. Trustees shall make annual reports to the reeves, accounting for all funds administered by them.

Paragraph 3. Care of the poor. The committees shall concern themselves with the care of the poor in accordance with the provisions of Chapter IV, Para. 5.

Paragraph 4. Responsibility for the building of meetinghouses. The committees shall promote construction by the residents of their respective districts of meetinghouses, in accordance with the provisions of Chapter IV, Para. 6.

Paragraph 5. Election of the Chairman of the Colony Council. All the committee members of each district shall have the responsibility of attending a meeting called for the purpose of electing a chairman and vice-chairman of the colony council. This meeting shall be held on the seventh day after the election of the district committees and shall be held one year at Lundur, the following year at Gimli.

Paragraph 6. Health regulations. The committees shall concern themselves with the state of health in their respective districts and take special measures to prevent the spread of contagious diseases when the occasion arises.

Paragraph 7. Encouraging fellowship and resolute action. The committee members of each district shall stimulate and encourage the residents of their districts to organize all kinds of societies and fellowships which will promote well-being and progress in the district.

1905, Icelandic pioneer woman spinning.

CHAPTER VII.

DUTIES OF REEVES, TREASURERS AND SECRETARIES.

A. Duties of the Reeves.

Paragraph 1. Calling meetings. Reeves shall summon the residents of their districts to the meetings designated in Chapter II and in Chapter IV, para. 1, and shall preside over them. They shall, in addition, summon the general public to extraordinary meetings when the committeemen see the necessity for them.

Paragraph 2. Committee meetings. They shall summon the members of their committees to meetings whenever necessary, and shall preside over such meetings.

Paragraph 3. Minute book. They shall ensure that the secretary records the minutes of all meetings in a book to be designated Book No. 1.

Paragraph 4. Recording of census figures and statistics. They shall annually record all census and statistical figures in a Book to be designated Book No. 2.

ORDER-IN-COUNCIL NO. 987, OCTOBER 8 1875

Creating Icelandic Reserve

On a memorandum dated 28th September 1875 from the Hon. Minister of the Interior submitting for consideration a letter dated 5th September 1875 of the Secretary of the Department of Agriculture and application of W. John Taylor, Icelandic agent, requesting that the Western coast of Lake Winnipeg extending from the mouth of the Red River on the south to a point known as Grindstone Point on the north including Big Black Island and all other islands adjacent within the miles of the said coast and extending from Lake Winnipeg on the east to Range Two East of the Principal Meridian on the West be an Icelandic reserve.

The Minister observes that as there are several homestead entries for lands in Township No.17 in the Fourth Range East and valuable lime and sandstone quarries between the Seventh Base Line and Big Grindstone Point, he recommends that the reserve for the Icelanders be for the present limited to the tract bounded to the South by the Northern boundaries of the Province of Manitoba, to the North by the Seventh Base Line, to the East by Lake Winnipeg, and to the West by the Eastern boundary of the Second Range East of the Principal Meridian embracing townships Nos. 18 to 24 inclusive in the Third and Fourth Ranges East, also Big Black Island and the small islands lying between it and the said coast as indicated on a map accompanying this Memorandum.

The Committee submits for Your Excellency's approval.
A. MacKenzie and Wm. G. Haley
Approved July 10, 1875

Paragraph 5. Record of road maintenance. They shall annually record all accounts of road construction and improvements in a book to be designated Book No. 3.

Paragraph 6. Record of deaths, births and marriages. They shall enter a record of all deaths, births and marriages which take place in their respective districts in a book designated Book No. 4.

Paragraph 7. Record of inventories of estates etc. They shall enter records of inventories, appraisals, auctions, transfers and ownership of property in a book, designated Book No. 5.

Paragraph 8. Attendance at meetings of the colony council. They shall attend all meetings of the colony council and acquaint the residents of their respective districts with the decisions they made at those meetings.

Paragraph 9. Inspection of official records and submission of reports. They shall bring with them for inspection all official records to the annual meeting of the colony council and shall submit to the chairman of the colony council annually, before the 7th of January, all the reports mentioned in Paragraphs 4, 5 and 6 of this chapter.

B. Duties of Treasurers

Paragraph 1. Administration of district and road assessments. Treasurers shall accept payment and call in amounts due to the district treasuries and funds for road maintenance, and shall make payments out of such funds after consultation with the reeves.

Paragraph 2. Records of income and expenditure. He shall keep regular accounts of income and expenditure, to be reviewed by the district committees at the end of each year.

C. Duties of Secretaries

Paragraph 1. Recording the minutes of meetings. The secretary shall record all that transpires at all committee meetings and public meetings.

Paragraph 2. Compilation of voters lists and election results. He shall prepare voters lists and ensure their correctness. He shall, moreover, accept and count the ballots in connection with all elections in the district as well as any referendum on proposals presented for the residents approval.

CHAPTER VIII.

DISPOSITION OF ESTATES AND THE PROCEEDS OF THEM.

Estates to which claim is made by minors who have lost their father or mother, or by persons not residing in New Iceland, shall be inventoried, appraised and sold at public auction, if necessity dictates, by the reeve of the district, and settled as expeditiously as possible, or within the next twelve-month period. In inventorying and appraising estates, the reeve shall be accompanied by two committeemen. For the inventory and appraisal of an estate a fee of 3% shall be levied; for an auction and the collection of its proceeds, 4%; for settlement, 3%; all of which shall apply to estates up to $500.00 in value; for estates valued between $500.00 and $1,000.00 the fees shall be 2% for inventory and appraisal, 3% for the auction and collection of proceeds and 2% for settlement or division. On estates exceeding $1,000.00 in value $1\frac{1}{2}$% shall be charged for inventory and appraisal, 2% for auction and collection, and $1\frac{1}{2}$% for settlement. The same proportionate charges shall be levied against all other auctions conducted by the reeves.

CHAPTER IX.

JURISDICTION OF UMPIRES AND MEDIATORS.

The duties of umpires consist of endeavouring to bring about the settlement of all private disputes. The umpires may summon the disputants to appear before them at a particular place on a designated day, at the request of either of the disputants, and an announcement in writing may constitute a proper summons. If no settlement is reached, the plaintiff shall pay each of the umpires the sum of one dollar for the attempt at reconciliation, but if the dispute is settled, each of the disputants shall pay the same amount after agreement is reached. Payment will be made at the conclusion of the attempt to effect reconciliation. The umpires have the responsibility of keeping a record of

settlements reached and their attempts to arrive at settlements. Should an attempt to reach a settlement be unsuccessful, or should one of the parties not meet with the other after the issuance of a lawful summons, the disputants shall be required, if either of them so wishes, to submit the matter to the mediation of five disinterested men, whom the disputants themselves shall reimburse. The disputants shall name two mediators each, while the fifth shall be the chairman or vice-chairman of the colony council, if the parties cannot agree on a fifth man. The outcome of cases shall be determined by majority vote. The mediators are required to keep written records of their proceedings.

CHAPTER X.

ENACTMENT OF ADDITIONAL LAWS BY THE DISTRICT COMMITTEES.

Each district committee shall formulate proposals for additonal laws regarding various matters affecting the

---

ORDER-IN-COUNCIL NO. 2306, OCTOBER 9 1897

Rescinding Order-in-Council No. 987

On a report dated 22nd July 1897, from the Minister of the Interior stating that by Order-in-Council of 8th October, 1875, a tract of land shown coloured pink on the annexed plan, and embracing Townships 18 to 24 inclusive in the third and fourth ranges east of the Principal Meridian, and also Black Island and the small islands lying between it and the western shore of Lake Winnipeg, was set apart as a Reserve for Icelanders. The Minister further states that by Order-in- Council of 29th May 1885, the exclusive privileges enjoyed by Icelanders of making entry for portions of the even numbered sections within this reserve was extended to the odd numbered sections as well for a period of two years from 1st June 1885, and by subsequent Orders the last of which bearing the date 7th January 1897, this privilege was extended up to the 31st of December 1898.

The Minister is of the opinion that the purpose for which this Reserve was made has now been fully served, and he recommends that the Order-in-Council of 8th October 1875, and subsequent Orders in that behalf be rescinded, and that the even and odd numbered sections remaining at the disposal of the government in the tract in question be thrown open for sale and homestead entry by any class of settlers who may wish to locate in that vicinity.

The Committee submits the above recommendation for Your Excellency's approval.
B.I. Cartwright
Approved July 30, 1897

district, such as, for example, regulations with regard to care of the indigent, fencing and personal responsibilities, the disposition of all livestock of questionable ownership etc., provided such laws do not conflict with the provisions of this constitution. These proposals shall be presented at public meetings to the eligible voters of the district for their approval. If a majority of the eligible voters of a district vote in favour of proposals, they acquire the authority of law.

CHAPTER XI.
COLONY COUNCIL AND CHAIRMAN OF THE COLONY COUNCIL.

Paragraph 1. Composition of the council. The Lake Settlement shall be governed by a committee of five men, to be known as the Colony Council. This council shall be composed of the reeves of the four districts of the settlement together with a man elected in accordance with the provisions of Chapter VI, para. 5, to be known as the Chairman of the Colony Council.

Paragraph 2. Election of the Chairman of the Colony Council. Everyone eligible for election to membership in a district committee is eligible for election to the positions of Chairman or Vice chairman of the Colony Council (See Chapter III). The duly elected Chairman of the Colony Council shall be he who receives a majority of the votes of all members of the district committees of the settlement. Should it transpire that no one receives a majority of the votes cast, then a firm decision shall be made between the two who have received the greatest number of votes. Should neither of these receive a majority, the incumbent Chairman shall retain his position until the next meeting held to elect his successor. The same rules shall apply to the election of the Vice-chairman. In the event either the Chairman or Vice-chairman declines to accept election at the meeting, another election shall be held. Should one of the reeves be elected Chairman of the Colony Council, he shall resign from his position as reeve before assuming responsibilities in the government of the colony.

CHAPTER XII.
MEETINGS OF THE COLONY COUNCIL.

The Colony Council shall hold one general meeting each year on the 10th day of March, or on the 11th, should the 10th fall on a Sunday. This meeting of the Colony Council shall be held at Gimli those years the election meetings are held at Lundur, and at Lundur those years election meetings are held at Gimli. In addition, the Chairman of the Colony Council shall call special meetings of the Council when necessary, at a place and time to be decided by him.

CHAPTER XIII.
JURISDICTION OF THE COLONY COUNCIL.

Paragraph 1. Jurisdiction of matters of interest to the entire colony and the enactment of supplemental laws. The Colony Council shall have jurisdiction over matters of concern to the colony as a whole which are in any way related to its future development, arranging for expansion of the colony's area, for instance, granting permission for native-born Canadians to settle in it, contracting for the establishment of advantageous enterprises etc. The Colony Council shall formulate proposals for supplemental laws regarding such matters, which the reeves shall have brought to a vote at public meetings, each in his own district. Those proposals approved by a majority of all eligible voters of the colony shall have the force of law.

Paragraph 2. Responsibility for maintaining a highroad as well as roads within each district. It shall assume the responsibility for constructing and maintaining the highroad of the colony, running from north to south, and of all roads running from east to west within each district, as well the necessary construction of bridges on these roads over rivers, creeks and marshes.

Paragraph 3. Inspection of record books. It shall inspect the record books of all the reeves, audit the account book of the Chairman of the Colony Council, and ensure their correctness.

Paragraph 4. Resolution of disputes between districts. It shall resolve disputes between districts, should they arise, or the cases may be mediated in the manner provided by the provisions applicable to private disputes, set forth in Chapter IX.

CHAPTER XIV.
JURISDICTION OF THE CHAIRMAN OF THE COLONY COUNCIL.

Paragraph 1. Calling meetings. The Chairman of the Colony Council shall call all meetings of the Council and preside over them. See Chapter XIII.

Paragraph 2. Minutes of meetings. He shall enter all minutes in a book, to be designated No. 1.

Paragraph 3. Recording and publication of a synopsis of district reports. He shall enter in a book, designated Book No. 2, an extract of all reports from the districts of the colony and issue a summary of it in print annually.

Paragraph 4. Recording of road reports and accounts. He shall enter in a book, designated Book No. 3, reports and accounts covering the maintenance of roads under the jurisdiction of the Colony Council, and present this report at the general meeting of the Colony Council.

Paragraph 5. Dealings with the Dominion Government. He shall communicate to the Dominion Government all those matters pertaining to the colony which need to be disclosed, and he shall advise the reeves of all decrees which affect the settlement.

Paragraph 6. Advising the reeves on various matters. He shall direct the attention of the reeves to those matters requiring discussion at meetings of the district committees and general meetings preparatory to action at a meeting of the Colony Council.

Paragraph 7. Participation in mediation committees. He shall participate in mediation committees in accordance with the provisions of Chapter IX. For each participation in such activity the Chairman of the Colony Council shall be entitled to a fee of five dollars.

Paragraph 8. Synopsis of the State of the Colony. At the meeting held to elect a new Chairman of the Colony Council he shall present a detailed report of his work the previous year, what has been done that affects the colony as a whole. He shall take its economy into account, shed light on its projects for the future, and recommend what, in his opinion, of general concern to the settlement needs to be done, and how he thinks it should best be accomplished.

CHAPTER XV.
AUTHORITATIVENESS OF ELECTIONS AND VOTES.

Election to all offices named in these laws is for a period of one year, but re-election is permitted. A majority of the votes cast shall determine all elections and decisions made at all meetings which these laws provide for.

CHAPTER XVI.
DEFRAYMENT OF COST OF WRITING MATERIALS AND BOOKS.

Upon presentation of correct invoices, the cost of writing materials, the books which the Chairman of the colony Council, reeves, treasurers and secretaries are required to keep, as well as all essential printing shall be defrayed from the district treasuries.

CHAPTER XVII.
WHEN THESE LAWS ENTER INTO EFFECT.

These laws enter into effect when they are published in print.

CHAPTER XVIII.
AMENDMENT OF THESE LAWS.

These laws may be amended by motions adopted at the general meeting of the Colony Council and later ratified by a majority of all eligible voters of the colony at meetings to be held in each district, all of which shall be held on the same day.

(Ratified at Gimli and Sandy Bar, January 11, 1878.)

Lord Dufferin's Visit

Adapted from an article by Halldór Briem in *Framfari,* Vol. 1, No. 3, November 17, 1877

Preparations consisted of clearing a rectangular area, about the size of a hay field that could be mown in a single day, at the so-called market place, clearing away all the tree trunks, brush and grass.

Rows of young spruce trees, about sixteen feet high, were placed along the fence as well as to the north. A platform was erected at the middle of the west side of the enclosure, eighteen feet wide, straight on the side facing the lake but curved on the west side. Fir trees were arranged to form an arch in front of the platform. A landing stage was erected out on the lake with a flight of steps up the bank.

The morning of the 14th the "Colville," decorated with many large and small flags, was seen again, steaming south along the lake, headed for the bay. The flags at Gimli were raised at once. His Lordship came ashore soon afterward just the same and was received at the landing stage by Mr. Taylor and Mr. Friðjón Friðriksson, who was to serve as his interpreter. The Governor-General and his retinue, consisting of Colonel Littleton, Captain Hamilton, Captain Smyth, his stenographer Mr. Campbell, and a reporter from the Toronto "Globe" walked around the entire community and visited every house. He inspected three farms and visited the homes of three farmers, Eggert Gunnlaugsson from Húsey, Jón Árnason from Máná, and Páll Jónsson. Everywhere he went he made painstaking enquiries of men's financial means and present situation, whether they were satisfied with their living conditions here and their hopes for the future. Everyone expressed his complete satisfaction.

He recalled his journey to Iceland in 1856 and how he wrote his book, *Letters from High Latitudes.* He was more complimentary to Icelanders than most foreigners who have visited their country and ever since has had a warm regard for Icelanders.

At 4 o'clock in the afternoon more than 100 Icelanders had gathered at Gimli and arranged themselves in a semi-circle in front of the platform. His Lordship then arrived and mounted the platform with his retinue. Mr. Friðjón Friðriksson then delivered an address in Icelandic, handing his Lordship an English translation of it. His Lordship replied to the address with the following words in English, which were translated simultaneously into Icelandic:

"During a hasty visit like the present I cannot pretend to acquire more than a superficial insight into your condition, but so far as I have observed, things appear to be going sufficiently well with you. The homesteads I have visited seem well built and commodious, and are certainly far superior to any of the farmhouses I remember in Iceland, while the gardens and little clearings which have begun to surround them show that you have already tapped an inexhaustible store of wealth in the rich alluvial soil on which we stand. The three arts most necessary to a Canadian colonist are the felling of timber, the plowing of land, and the construction of highways, but as in your own country no one of you had ever seen a tree, a cornfield, or a road, it is not to be expected that you should immediately exhibit any expertness in these accomplishments, but practice and experience will soon make you the masters of all three, for you possess in a far greater degree than is probably imagined that which is the essence and foundation of all superiority – intelligence, education, and intellectual activity. In fact I have not entered a single hut or cottage in the settlement which did not contain, no matter how bare its walls or scanty its furniture, a library of twenty or thirty volumes; and I am informed that there is scarcely a child amongst you who cannot read and write. Secluded as you have been for hundreds of years from all contact with the civilization of Europe, you may in many respects be a little rusty and behind the rest of the world; nor perhaps have the conditions under which you used to live at home – where months have to be spent in the enforced idleness of a sunless winter – accustomed you to those habits of continued and unflagging industry which you will find necessary to your new existence; but in our brighter, drier, and more exhilarating climate you will become animated with fresh vitality, and your continually expanding prosperity will encourage you year by year to still greater exertions.

And remember that in coming amongst us you will find yourselves associated with a race both kindly hearted and cognate to your own, nor in becoming Englishmen and subjects of Queen Victoria need you forget your own time-honored customs or the picturesque annals of your forefathers. On the contrary, I trust you will continue to cherish for all time the heart-stirring literature of your nation, and that from generation to generation your little ones will continue to learn in your ancient Sagas that industry, energy, fortitude, perseverance, and stubborn endurance have ever been the characteristics of the noble Icelandic race."

Thereupon several of the most prominent men of the colony were presented to him. He shook hands with them and had a few friendly words for each one. Then he went to the audience arranged in a semi-circle and greeted everyone he could reach with a handshake. He asked all kinds of questions about their living conditions and how they liked being here and they all told him they considered it their good fortune to have come here. By and large His Lordship displayed a degree of concern, courtesy and kindness that is probably to be found but rarely among the upper classes. One of the Icelandic girls was in holiday

Steina Vidal rowing out to a big rock.

dress and many of the women wore everyday Icelandic dress of homespun. He was especially taken by the festive dress and expressed his hope that the womenfolk would not abandon it. In conversation with individuals here, Lord Dufferin also disclosed his delight over the accomplishments of the Icelanders here in so short a time, and mentioned that he found their housing and all their living conditions far better than he had expected. He was also favourably impressed by the land and declared that despite the adversities the Icelanders had encountered here previously, there was no doubt that the future was promising for them. At 6 o'clock he bade farewell to the Icelanders and left to board his ship. A boat was dispatched from the "Colville" to take him out to the ship, but Jane and Susan Taylor offered to row him out in a little boat which they owned, and he gladly accepted their offer. Lord Dufferin's visit was the occasion of the greatest festivity our colony has yet seen. The weather was the finest possible, with sunshine and calm, the lake as smooth as a mirror. Gimli made so wonderfully attractive an appearance in its holiday garb that no one could imagine who had seen it a year previously. Lord Dufferin found its appearance most attractive and made pencil sketches of the reception area and of Willow Point.

1901, The Gimli school.

The Smallpox Letter, March 13, 1877

Augustus Baldwin, M.D.
The somewhat erratic spelling and grammar of the original letter has been maintained.

My darling Phoebe

I am going to fulfil my promis. That was as soon as I got back to Winnipeg. I was to write and tell you all I did during the winter. I left this on Sunday the 26th of November – I got up to Gimli the next day – in the evening. Next morning, I went over with Dr. Lynch – to visit the Hospital. It was full of patients, of course all with small pox. They were to be seen in every stage, some dieing – and some convalescent. The next day, I went to visit several houses and such a sight you never saw – Every house had somebody down with the disease – The settlement extends about forty five Miles. And the houses were of the worst discription. I had to stoop to go into nearly every house – There were some doors so low, that I had to go on my hands and knees to get in – And such filth. I cannot describe it – And fancy, I had to sleep in these wretched houses. I always slept with my clothes on, so that I would not get lice on me. I wore a leather coat. The houses are all one room. And in some there would be 18 or 19 in them. They would all be huddled together like so many pigs – And then those houses that had room, they would have their cows in them – I had to sleep several times in the same house in which they had their cows at the other end of the room – in which I was sleeping – You can imagin that it would not smell very sweet – And one of the cows were neigh hir accouchement – And the way she would grunt and groan. She would not let me sleep very much –

On my first trip, when I was forty miles north of Gimli – on one of those large Islands – my guide took the small pox. Well as he and I used the same blankits, we slept together and I had to sleep with him and he with the eruption out on him – for four nights. At the end of that time I was able to get another guide. And then started across again to White Mud River, but night – and a storm over took us before we could reach the land – and we could not see where to go to – And here we were out on the Lake, and no shelter – I quite made up my mind that I would loose either my feet or hands, as the place was about forty below zero and no way to get warm – But at

1882, Homestead of Friðfinnur Johnson in Argyl.

last my guide found land, with some ded willows – so we set to work and made a fire. And I had to put one of my blankets on the horse, to keep him warm. And then the other I put it a bar to keep the wind off our backs, and then we had nothing to put over ourselves. We took turn about to cut wood for the fire. We had to keep so close to the fire that the sparks were always shooting on us, so you can imagin what a night we had to put in. And it was storming the whole night. – When we got the fire well made, Then we had to think of geting some tea, so we had the kettle filled with snow and put on – so we had out tea made – and then we had to put out our dry pemacann, And set to work as that was all we had. And then Breakfas, next morning was the same – and dinner too. But the poor horse had to fair worse. We could not even get the proor brute a drink of water – As the Ice was solid down to the ground – and it was too cold to go out on the lake, if we did, we would had our fingers frozen –

It began to clear up about 4 o'clock, so we thought it was time to get out of that cold place. We arrived at Sandy Bar and stoped in a tent that night – with some surveyors. Then the next day the storm contiued so we had to stay till Sunday. And after Breakfast we started for White Mud River. And in the eveing I felt as if I was in for an attc of my old complaint which shure enough next morning I was compelled to stay in bed. And Remained there for a week. On the second day I left for Gimli, and it was frightfully cold – but it did not do me any hard. I got back two days before Christmas day. And had my Xmas dinner in a tent. I could not help thnking what a difference it was to last Xmas. When I was at dear old home with you all, having such a jolly time. Then on NewYear's day – I was on my second trip on the Lake going my round trip again – on my third trip I had to amputate three feet that got badly frozen – The poor devils go lost on the Lake in a storm. One has no Idea what a storm is on the Lake unless they have been in one themselves. Lake Winnipeg is very large –

For three months I did nothing but treat for small pox – so you can imagin that I have seen enough of it – When I went to some of the houses, I would find perhaps some six or eight sick, some that had only a few hours to live – You would see Old Men and woman, Young men and girls, and poor little infants that would make the hardest heart ache for them, and to see them at their Mother's breast and prhaps the next time I came around their little bodies would be put out side till they had time to make a rough box to bury them in. On my second trip I hear that there was a family on Big Black Island. So I went to see them. And such a sight. The Mother had just got over the small pox and her infant at her brest, dieing and they had not a thing to cover the poor thing – The house was so small that I could not stand up in it. I was compeled to sit down. I brought my tea and pemacan, and me and my Indian guide had to have our dinner on that a lone – after a whole days travel – They had no flour infact, had nothing but fish – I left what medicine and nurishment I had – which I brought for the sick – and to see their eyes brighten up, to hopes that it came in time to save their little one can never be forgoten – But alas, the little thing only nine months old, died next day. And then they had to put the little thing on top of the house till they could get some boards to make a box for the little one – I had a pretty hard time myself, but when I looked at the poor Icelanders I faired like a King – Though I had to sleep on a bed of hay – No body, but one that has a strong stomach could have eaten what I did this winter, unless they were the Icelanders them-selves – In one house a woman asked me if I would have a cup of coffee. I said yes, as the day was cold, so while I ws making up some medicine for a poor sick boy – What do you think I saw the woman do – She no doubt thought that the cup was not clean enough for me, so she licked the cup all around with hir tongue and then took a towel as balck as it could be – without it being a bit of black coth and dryed with it, and then gave it to me to drink. A nice sight to see for a man that wanted a drink to warm him. I could tell you worse than this. And then to finish up with, when I came back to Winnipeg I had to put in my Quarantine which was 15 days, as I had not had the small pox – well before I had quite put in all my time, I was put in charge of the Hospital at Netley Creek – And when there I lived in a house that only two Rooms. And I boarded in one room with the man and his son for 6 dollars a week, And the other room was a place where they had about two dozen chickens, one doz. geese, one doz. Ducks, and some guinea Fowl, And some wild geese that he had tamed. And such a noise you never heard. And some times he would sing. And came through it all safe and sound – without any harm, or small pox, while the other three Medical Men all got the small pox –

Now my darling Phoebe I think that I have not done so bad. And I think that you will say what a goose I was to write such stuff – But this will have to do for a year –

It is my wish to wish you all a Happy Year – Father & Mother, brother & sister one and all – Nephews and Neice. And hope that you are all quite well, I am A No. 1. Oh! it was great fun someone started the rumor that I had to cut off my beard – so as not to bring any small pox to Town. Well if you only heard exclamations of all, it was fun – And then Wehn I came back to see the people all congratulated me on not loosing my beard. My beard is the beard of the whole Province. And it is still larger then when I was down. Every one tell me that I am looking very well after my hard winter, I wish that I could take a run down to see you all – There is nothing new about the Town, we still have sleighing. What a beautiful weather we had last month – I had a letter from Aunt Georgina the other day asking me if I could do something for Frank Whitla, and also from Frank himself – I am shure he will not know what to make of me in the way I adressed him for the first time. He adressed me in his letter as A. Baldwin Esq. M.D. – then Sir. So I just told him not to do so again, but just put plain Guss, I told him that if he only knew me, he would have known better, and the sooner he did know me the better, I feel sorry for him – I told him that I would do all I could for him. There are two more Baldwins in Town now from England, and the other day I got a letter from one of their lady friends. And I read it all and had it in my pocket for a month before I know that there were any B. here beside myself – I was very sorry to hear that poor Norman was so ill.

After returning from such a long visit to this out of the way place – I missed seeing Jim McL. and his wife – But I believe that they will soon be back. Well I must now close so good by – and love to all, and a kiss for my boy – hoping that he is quite well, love to all at Mashquotch – and St. G.B. & Amelia.

I remain your most affect. Brother
Augustus B

The steamer "Tempest" at Gull Harbour.

A Few Hints to Icelandic Emigrants

Jóhann Briem
Framfari, Vol. I. No. 7, January 4, 1878

There are numerous indications that interest in emigrating to America is continuing to grow in Iceland. Since no advice or hints with regard to preparations for leaving home or various aspects of the journey have appeared in print for the benefit of those leaving , I should like to touch, briefly on several matters in this connection that I think many people will find helpful.

Emigration to America – the words sound the same wherever they are spoken in Iceland, but they do not convey the same meaning. This land is enormous.

Imported Icelandic ponies in Framnes, Manitoba.

Opportunities for employment and making a livelihood differ widely depending upon what part of America a man comes to and what he decides to do with his life after he is here. As far as Icelandic laymen are concerned, one need not take into consideration a variety of choices apart from the fact that some acquire land and begin to farm, while others work for wages for farmers already established here, or for railroads, factories or wherever else they can earn the highest wages being paid at the time. At this point I am unable to give men dependable advice from my own experience as to whether farming or working for wages is preferable in the beginning. That depends largely upon the circumstances and capabilities of each individual. There is much, however, to suggest that farming is productive of better results than day labour, even more so since farmers can seek seasonal work even though they have land under cultivation, and most people tend to take up land in the very beginning, for after land has been cultivated to some extent, it is considered to be the soundest and most profitable possession an impecunious immigrant can expect to own. But whether an emigrant takes up a homestead or not, he needs to familiarize himself with everything that could provide him with an example to be followed or a warning, before he makes up his mind to emigrate and before setting out on the journey he needs to prepare himself more or less for the way of life he has determined to follow. It should be obvious that a man who plans to move around wherever the highest wages are paid should bring fewer possessions with him than a man who plans to settle down at once to farming, for removals from place to place are expensive everywhere.

Since I anticipate that by far the largest number of emigrants will in future as in the past turn to farming, and aware that opinions will differ, I would none the less direct my words to those who intend to settle down as farmers, anywhere in America, but particularly in this colony, where I know the conditions best.

Although old Iceland and New Iceland are two dissimilar lands and people can in no respect expect to farm here as they do at home, yet in many ways they can profitably have use of various implements and tools which are commonly employed in Iceland. It is just as essential to have some of them here and it is doubtful, moreover, whether the owners would receive full value, were they sold at home. The principal implements and tools I would advise immigrants to America to bring with them are: all implements connected to the blacksmith's trade, most of the tools used by carpenters, such as the iron items customarily found on a joiner's bench, clamps or the tools to fabricate them, cross-cut saws, various kinds of blades for frame-saws, carpenter's adzes, hand braces, files, pincers, chisels, blades for planes, and even good plane stocks. It would also be advantageous if someone brought with him machine shop items not made of wood, as well as cutting edges for lathes. It is also good to have the iron components of looms and all kinds of good weaving implements, those not constructed of wood, likewise all implements used in the manufacture of wool yarn, spinning wheels and combs, for instance. Many of these implements and tools are not available in this country and those that are are far more expensive (than at home). I should also advise those intending to come here to provide themselves with a good supply of clothing, especially underwear and socks; also with as many bedclothes as they need for themselves and their dependents; in addition, a considerable quantity of wool for making repairs to clothing as well as leather for shoes, smithy-bellows etc. Then there are also other items it would not be out of the way to bring over if one has room for them in his baggage,

binding materials, for instance, such as straps or ropes twisted from horsehair, and various other possessions which would bring little if sold, but are neither too large nor too heavy to bring along. In this respect emigrants can make up their minds according to circumstances and personal inclinations. If they have room in their baggage,

Harvesting ice at Gimli.

I would also recommend that they bring with them all the books they own. I would in no way discourage them, but in every way encourage them to bring as many books as possible, on both spiritual and worldly matters.

The chests in which an emigrant packs his belongings need to be good and strong with good locks. To make all old chests more secure they should be reinforced with iron at the corners and underneath. It is also necessary to have a handle of twisted rope or iron at each end of the chests and they must be clearly marked with the owner's name, with care taken that the name cannot be rubbed or blotted off.

It is inconvenient to have chests that are too large and

c. 1905 The children of W.B. (Vladimar Bjornsson) Gislason,
dressed in their Victorian best. Photo courtesy Bill Holm.

equally inconvenient to have them too small. The most suitable size is that of the "half chests" made in Iceland (these were provided with a convex lid and were narrower at the bottom than at the top) and they should not weigh more than 150-200 pounds, so that two men can easily carry them. Strong sacks may be used for the shipment of soft articles, such as comforters, feathers, wool, skins etc. In addition to the large chests used for shipping personal belongings people also need to have small chests and hand luggage in which to keep the items they will need daily on the journey, for people seldom have access to the bulk of their baggage which is stowed in the holds of ships and in special cars on railways.

I would also advise emigrants to take with them sufficient Icelandic food, for experience has shown the food people eat along the way to disagree with them, to say nothing of other changes which are inescapable. This food ought to consist especially of hardfish, butter or good mutton, tallow kæfa (a kind of seasoned meat pâté), smoked lamb and biscuits; in addition, pure and good sour whey, rock candy, and a little good akvavit made from grain. Of all these items, particularly the last mentioned, it is necessary to have more than will be consumed on the sea journey. It would not be amiss, however, to have a little more food.

I will not omit advising all prospective emigrants to have themselves vaccinated before setting out, for experience has shown us in a particularly painful way how dangerous it is to neglect that. It is truly astonishing how the officials of the country who ought to be concerned with such matters are, or have been, remiss in their duties. One could also cite instances even of clergymen providing birth certificates for children before they left, but disregarding the fact that they had not been vaccinated. It is tragic that the Alþing, while playing the quack by passing legislation related to emigration, should have neglected altogether dealing with the subject of vaccination, for vaccination protects that which is most precious, the health and life of human beings. In view of the importance of vaccination to the emigrants and the general heedlessness which has been manifest in official circles recently, there is every reason for the prospective emigrants themselves to assume the responsibility of having themselves vaccinated.

Furthermore, I would recommend that in order to prevent seasickness and the stomach disorders that plague travellers to the west as a consequence of the change of air and food, they take a laxative before boarding the ship as well as from time to time during the sea voyage.

With respect to the transfer of funds, there is less difficulty now that gold coinage has been introduced in Iceland than formerly when the old silver coinage circulated there exclusively. Under the present circumstances it is therefore easier for emigrants to bring with them the greater part of their capital in gold, but whether they have Danish gold or silver, they should be prepared to accept a discount for English gold currency or dollars. It goes without saying that English gold currency is more highly valued here than Danish; an English pound sterling is worth four dollars and eighty six cents here, while 20 gold crowns brings five dollars. The Danish Rijksdollar, or two crowns, is worth fifty cents here in Canada, with shillings and aurar in the same proportion. It is self evident that an emigrant would leave money or property behind in Iceland only to an individual in whom he had complete confidence and to arrange for the most expeditious transfer of funds.

The most dependable method for most people to transfer assets from Iceland is, in my opinion, to make arrangements with the directors or managers of the Gránufélag to deposit their funds with the association so the Board of Directors can then purchase a letter of credit for the amount at one of the banking houses in Copenhagen, this letter to be drawn on the Bank of Montreal in that city, which will then pay to the owner of the letter the amount indicated in it. Letters of credit drawn on the Bank of Montreal can be redeemed anywhere in Canada; there is a branch of the bank in Winnipeg.

SIMON SIMONSON

About midnight the people were dumped out of the wagons, under the trees, in darkness such as I have scarcely seen the like. We knew not where to go, and had the sick children on our hands. At last, after a long and distressing wait, with the people milling about in the mud, two of our countrymen came, bringing a faint light, and directed us to a hovel which was under construction, and at the building of which a few Icelanders worked.

Tired and hungry, we arrived at these miserable quarters. There was some food on the table, but only the strongest secured this, while the weak and the sick received nothing. Each thought of self, and no one else. I could not bring myself to act like a wild beast.

Sygtryggur's plan was to have a communal table, with all alike sharing expenses. His system, however, did not do so well, and there were those who pilfered supplies. . . . I do not care to describe it now, after twenty years; this was an unhappy period of my life. Also, we had to wait for our bed-comforters several days. All this was hard on the children, who were continuously taking ill. As for the men, they were unused to the work, and all were ignorant of the language. Most bitter of all, for me, was to see my little Guðrún suffering intensely and to be unable to ease her suffering. She kept nothing down. There was little milk to be had and what little there was, was not good. About nine days from the time Guðrún became ill, God took her to himself, in his merciful embrace. She died at ten o'clock in the evening of Saturday, the eighteenth of October. Jón Ívarson made the coffin. She was buried on the twentieth, in Kinmount cemetery. Jón and Jakob Espolin dug the grave and were pall-bearers. Guðrún was a lovely and pleasant child, well developed for her years, and appeared to be endowed with good intelligence. I shall mourn the loss of my loved one as long as I live.

–from "Reminiscences of Simon Simonson," trans. by William Kristjánson, *The Icelandic Canadian,* Winter, 1946

Journeys of Icelanders to America

Jóhann Briem
Framfari, Vol.1 No. 5, December 10, 1877

I want to mention as briefly as possible the reasons which first impelled Icelanders to emigrate from Iceland to any extent. It may be that some found unendurable the many kinds of blunders, burdensome taxes and other unjust treatment on the part of the government, just as their forefathers in Norway, about a thousand years ago. It is also not unlikely that the inclemency of the Icelandic climate affected emigration from there. It may also be that some people emigrated without giving the matter much thought, perhaps under the impression that all their problems would thereby be solved. Whatever the reasons may

have been at first, within approximately six years, or since 1871, almost two thousand people have emigrated from Iceland to America, but very few have probably gone to other countries. The first sizeable group of people, from northern Iceland, left the summer of 1873 on the horse transport "Queen." The summer of 1874 about 250 people also left from the north on the S.S. "St. Patrick," which was the first ship to carry passengers directly from Iceland to America. Both these groups, as well as those who had come to America earlier, spread far and wide upon their arrival. Nearly half of those who left Iceland in 1873 went

1915, Mundi Johnson and dog team.

to Wisconsin in the United States, the others to Ontario. All of the latter group settled in Ontario. In the year 1875 there was virtually no emigration from Iceland to America. Those who were already here, on the other hand, moved around a good deal that year. About 60 of the ones in Ontario moved to Nova Scotia with the intention of establishing an Icelandic colony there. Many, however, were of the opinion that on account of the space available and the quality of the land in Manitoba, it would be most expedient to establish an Icelandic colony there. Those who held the latter view sent two men to look over the land there in the west and select an area for a colony if they considered the land suitable for this purpose. The men sent to look over the land, who found no suitable location for a colony in Manitoba, selected a site just north of the provincial boundary, along Lake Winnipeg (the next largest lake in America) and named their colony "New Iceland." That district was then in the so called "Northwest Territory," but last winter a large area of the aforementioned territory was legally separated from it and is now called "The District of Keewatin." New Iceland is therefore now in Keewatin. After the exploring party had completed their work and returned east to Ontario, about 250 people decided to leave at once that autumn to settle their colony. They left Ontario at the end of September and reached their colony the last day of summer, 1875 (i.e. in mid-October, according to the old Icelandic reckoning of time). Since the season was so advanced, they were unable to move out into the countryside and take up homesteads. Most of them therefore settled in at one location in the southern part of the colony. They built temporary houses there and called their settlement "Gimli." About the same time this group set out from Ontario, the Dominion Government sent two of its agents to Iceland to offer those men there, who were thinking of emigrating, land in New Iceland, to provide those who wanted to emigrate with their passage and look after them on the journey. It is generally known that these agents were W. C. Krieger and Sigtryggur Jónasson. The former arrived in Iceland in October and the latter in December, 1875. They travelled extensively through Iceland the winter of 1876. A number of narrow-minded officials and other people who sympathized with them made all kinds of attempts, some of which were less than honourable, to hinder emigration, but their efforts had little effect, for the following summer about twelve hundred people in all emigrated from Iceland to America.

These people left Iceland in three parties. The first group, composed of 752 people from northern and western Iceland, sailed from Akureyri July 2nd on the S.S. "Verona," which arrived at Granton on the sixth of that month, proceeding thence without delay to Glasgow. From Glasgow the group sailed on the 11th on the S.S. "Austrian" of the Allan Line, arriving safely at Quebec on July 22nd. Nearly half of these people had decided to go to Nova Scotia, despite the fact that the provincial government had warned people, first in Iceland and then in Glasgow, that it was prepared to accept only a few families. Then on the way up the St. Lawrence River an agent of the Nova Scotia Government boarded the ship and, for the same reasons, recommended that only a few families consider going there. Accompanying the agent was an Icelander, Ólafur Brynjúlfsson from Bólstaðarhlíð, who had spent some time in Nova Scotia. He spoke deprecatingly of the circumstances in which his countrymen found themselves there on account of unemployment and the lack of fish, and read a letter, signed by ten Icelanders who were living there, strongly dissuading the immigrants from going to Nova Scotia. At this point the Dominion Government offered to relieve the provincial government of Nova Scotia of the responsibility for those who had intended to settle there, and to extend to them the same conditions and privileges offered to those who had decided to settle in New Iceland, both on the journey and afterward. The great majority accepted this offer with alacrity and only seven men went to Nova Scotia. The others, remaining together in a cohesive

PÖNNUKÖKUR

Sweet crêpes.

To make:
Beat together 2 eggs, ½ teaspoon vanilla and 2½ cups milk. In another bowl mix 1½ cups flour, 1½ teaspoons baking powder, ½ teaspoon cinnamon, ⅓ cup sugar and a pinch of salt. Pour wet ingredients into a hollow in dry ingredients. Mix well until smooth. Fry on a hot, lightly buttered surface, about ⅕th of a cup per crêpe.

In Canada and the United States, pönnukökur are usually sprinkled with brown sugar, rolled tightly, and cut in half. In Iceland they are usually filled with whipped cream and fruit and folded in four. They work well with any dessert crêpe recipe.

Sigurrós Vídal, R.N.
The first Public Health Nurse in the New Iceland area.

the evening of August 1st, then left there by train on the third and arrived at Fisher's Landing on the fourth. From there they began their journey north along the Red River the next day in a steamboat which had two other large boats attached to it, one on each side, arriving at Winnipeg on the 8th of August. Quite a few single men and women as well as a few families stayed behind in Winnipeg and found employment there. Those who planned to settle in the colony left Winnipeg on the 14th in accordance with the arrangements the government had made for them. Since people had with them a very large amount of personal property that could not be handled in small boats, it was loaded into several large flat bottomed vessels called flatboats, which it is customary to use for the transport of freight on the Red River. Since these have no motive power other than the current, they did not arrive at the mouth of the river before the 17th and then, on account of a headwind on Lake Winnipeg, had to wait there until the 19th and 20th before leaving again, but they arrived at the colony the same day.

A second group, comprising 399 individuals, which left Iceland the same summer departed from Seyðisfjörður on the 12th of July, also on the "Verona." This group had a somewhat easier time of it, for they did not have to wait nearly so long for ships and trains, and arrived at the colony at almost the same time.

The third and final group which left Iceland the same summer, composed of about twenty people from the southern part of the country, arrived at the colony a little later than the others.

Although the journey from Old Iceland to New Iceland took a long time, it could not be said to have been too unpleasant, even though there were many factors which might be attributed to the large number of people or to overcrowding on ships and railway carriages, as well as to unfamiliar food, which caused serious gastric disorders, especially among children, which is estimated to have caused the death of 30 to 40 of them. There were two

group, left Quebec by train on July 23rd, arriving at Toronto on the 24th. The group remained there until the 27th, then travelled by train to Collingwood and Sarnia, leaving there on the 28th by steamboats and continuing northwest across Lakes Huron and Superior. They were reunited in Duluth accidental deaths on the journey. Two men fell overboard from boats on the Red River and drowned. One was Pálmi Jónsson from Skagafjörður, an elderly and infirm man. He was a well-spoken and learned man who had a considerable knowledge of homeopathic medicine. The other man was with the last group, Sigurður Hjálmarsson from Skagafjörður, young and promising, who had taken up carpentry, and in that respect as well as others surpassed many of his own age.

This past summer about 50 more people emigrated from Iceland. Most of them were from the eastern part of the country, travelling by horse transport to Scotland, thence to Quebec. The larger part of this group settled in Minnesota, but some of them travelled all the way to New Iceland. They had an excellent journey.

STATE OF HEALTH AMONG THE ICELANDERS

Since the Icelanders came to the colony the state of health can under no circumstances be considered good. The winter of 1875-76 there was a great deal of sickness among our countrymen. One of the most serious ailments was scurvy, from which several people died. There were several other fatal illnesses in addition. In September 1876 there appeared among the Icelanders a dangerous and repulsive disease which soon spread throughout almost the entire colony. This disease, which no one recognized at first, proved to be smallpox. It was apparently not of the most dangerous variety, even though it affected approximately two thirds of the people in each of the infected dwellings. The smallpox raged for six months from the time it first appeared until it disappeared completely. Among the Icelanders there were 102 deaths, mostly of children and youths. The smallpox spread only a little during the first six weeks, but then it reached epidemic proportions. The provincial government of Manitoba, which is also the highest authority in Keewatin, then established a quarantine, enforced by soldiers, to prevent communications between New Iceland and Manitoba. This quarantine was set up on November 27th. A little later, around the beginning of December, at the instigation of the government agents here, there arrived a single physician to investigate the state of health and treat the sick. About the same time the provincial government sent two additional physicians for the same purpose, but unfortunately their remedies were unsuccessful, so their arrival and presence here were not of much benefit. Before the arrival of the physicians, arrangements were completed for the preparation of a hospital where the sick could be treated. A new warehouse, 40 feet long by 16 wide, which the government arranged to have built at Gimli was used for this purpose. At this hospital many were provided with far better nursing care than they would otherwise have had. All or some of these physicians were here for a period of three to four months. The fourth doctor came to replace all the others. He arrived here a short time before they left and remained here until early June. It was mentioned above that the quarantine was set up on November 27th; the quarantine station was established about 15 miles away, at the southern end of the colony along the so-called Netley Creek. No one who had not had the disease was permitted farther south unless he waited there 15 days, bathed and donned clean clothing, but those who had had smallpox were permitted to proceed without delay after taking a bath and changing their clothes. No letters were permitted to leave the colony without first being disinfected of possible contamination by being dipped in carbolic acid.

Long after the epidemic was over the Manitoba Government still did not consider it safe to assume that the smallpox infection had been eradicated. They had insufficient funds to maintain the quarantine as long as they would have liked, and the Dominion Government refused to appropriate money to maintain it. Finally an agreement was reached between the agents of the Dominion Government here and the provincial government of Manitoba to the effect that some kind of disinfection should be continued

RÚLLUPYLSA

Chop 5 large onions finely and mix with ½ cup salt, 1½ teaspoons saltpetre, 2 tablespoons allspice, 1 tablespoon pepper and 1 tablespoon cloves. This forms the filling. Trim most of the fat from ten de-boned lamb flanks. Trim the fat under the skin but do not remove the skin. Spread a thin layer of the mixture over the flanks, and under the flaps of meat as well. Roll tightly and wind with string. Sew the ends closed with string and a needle. Wrap tightly in plastic and place in plastic bags. Store in the refrigerator for one week. Remove from the plastic and simmer for approx. 2½ hours or until the meat is tender to a fork. Press the rúllupylsa under a weight until thorougly cooled. Serve sliced on Icelandic brown bread.

here in the colony: the dwellings of all Icelanders should be washed inside with slaked lime, all bedding and furnishings washed in boiling soapy water, with eiderdowns and other items that could not be washed without being damaged fumigated in sulphur fumes. This disinfection was carried out between June 8th and 20th under the supervision of Mr. Drever, who had been assistant to the physicians. Some time after the disinfection had been completed, the quarantine was finally lifted on the 20th of July.

ACCIDENTS

There have been few serious mishaps among the Icelanders since they settled in New Iceland. The summer before last a certain Jón Þorkelsson from Klúka died after eating a root he mistook for angelica root. Late last winter an elderly widow, Anna Guðmundsdóttir, from Steðji in Þelamörk, died of exposure on Lake Winnipeg. It can also be reckoned among the mishaps that last December two men from Big Island who were returning from Gimli in cruel weather were badly frost bitten. They had wet feet, lost their way, and were on their third day of suffering exposure. One of them had to have both feet amputated, the other only one. In the autumn of last year Þorsteinn Sigfússon from Hvammur in Möðruvellir sustained a broken leg when a tree fell on him and he has had a great deal of pain in it ever since. Early in August this summer a young boy drowned in Lake Winnipeg, Hjörtur Jóhannsson, who has relatives in Vatnsnes. He was practising swimming and probably had a cramp. Early in September a bachelor, Valdimar Sigmundsson from Þingeyjarsýsla, also drowned in Lake Winnipeg. He fell overboard from a sailboat and could not be rescued.

Fishing boats under sail on Lake Winnipeg.

Jón Bjarnason

Ingthor Isfeld

Pastor Bjarnason, or Séra Jón, as he was most often referred to, was without a doubt one of the most able and best educated ministers in Iceland in the 1880s. His mother, Rósa, was the daughter of the Rev. Brynjólfur Gíslason at Eydalir, Breiðdalur, Eastern Iceland. There had been Lutheran ministers in her family almost every generation since the Reformation. She was a descendant of Rev. Einar Sigurðsson (1539-1626) who is one of the better-known hymn writers in Icelandic Church history.

Rósa was a widow with eight children when she married Bjarni Sveinsson. Bjarni was a young farmer, an exceptionally bright man, a poet, well-versed in Greek and Roman literature. He had read all the writings of Plato in the original Greek and was fluent in Latin. Jón was born November 15, 1845, the eldest of three sons of Rósa and Bjarni. Two years later his father was ordained into the ministry, and served country parishes in the East of Iceland.

As a boy, Jón was fascinated by the classical sagas and so impressed by the Passion Hymns by Hallgrímur Pétursson that he committed many of them to memory. He got some schooling but was mostly taught by his father. By the age of 15 Jón was quite well versed both in Latin and Greek. In the fall of 1861, when Jón was not quite 16 years old, he was sent to Reykjavík to enter the Latin School, or college.

The spirit of the Latin School was not at all to Jón's liking. He was in many ways quite mature and even at this early age had a tendency to take life very seriously. He found the students irresponsible, the religious exercises superficial, and he felt that there was a lot of intellectual snobbery and atheistic tendencies associated with the school. He felt lonely and like a misfit, and this attitude of critical alienation from the educated class in

Rev. Jon Bjarnason, first minister in New Iceland.

Iceland seems to have remained with him most of his life.

After finishing the Latin School Jón went to the Seminary in Reykjavík and graduated from there in 1869, receiving the highest marks granted by that school up to that time. In the spring of 1869 he was ordained to be the assistant to his father, who was ill at the time. In a year his father's health improved and Jón returned to Reykjavík. He married Lára Mikaelína Guðjónsen on November 15, 1870, his 25th birthday. She was the eldest of 15 children of Pétur Guðjónsen and Sigríður Knudsen. Her father was a pioneer in the music life of Reykjavík and her mother came from a Danish family. The home was renowned for its culture and Lára was well-educated and used to hard work and frugality.

Jón earned a living for three years in Reykjavík by teaching, applying twice for a parish, but unsuccessfully. In 1873 the young couple started to think about going to America. They received letters from a young theological student, Páll Thorláksson who had already made the move. Páll told Jón that he would have a good chance of getting a parish among Norwegians, who were moving in droves to America at the time. They decided to go.

They left Reykjavík on September 5, 1873 and arrived in Quebec City three weeks later and left immediately for Milwaukee in Wisconsin. From there they went to St. Louis, Missouri to meet with Páll Thorláksson who was studying theology at a Missouri Synod Lutheran Seminary in that city.

They stayed in St. Louis for three weeks and then went to Decorah, Iowa, where the headquarters of the Norwegian Synod were located. They were well received by leaders of the Norwegian Synod and in a few months a whole new world opened up to Séra Jón. He was very impressed by the vitality of the church life among the Germans and the Norwegians and attributed this to the fact that these were free churches not dependent on the state. But quite soon Séra Jón found out that he could not work with the Norwegians. They found him too liberal and would not let him preach, and he found them too stringent in many ways. By January 1874 he was offered a position as a teacher in the Norwegian College in Decorah because, though the Norwegians did not like Jón's theology, they much admired his great learning. He taught Latin, Greek and Geography and was thought to be a very good teacher.

In 1874 there was a great national celebration in Iceland to commemorate the 1,000 years of settlement of the country. In the summer of 1874 a group of Icelandic immigrants were gathered in Milwaukee and they decided to have a celebration of their own. The celebration was held in a park on August 2nd with quite a few Norwegians taking part. As a part of this celebration the group gathered in a Norwegian Lutheran Church for the first Icelandic service in North America. Séra Jón conducted the service and preached on the 90th Psalm. This, incidentally, was the text on which the Icelandic National Anthem is based. The pastor and poet Matthías Jochumson had written the words to the anthem and he and Séra Jón were friends from school in Reykjavík.

Séra Jón was soon hired as the editor of the Norwegian paper, *Skandinavien,* in Chicago. He did not like that and then became the editor of another Norwegian paper, *Budstikken,* in Minneapolis. He liked the work, was well-paid and the circulation of the paper increased greatly under his leadership. His future in the U.S. looked very bright.

But then came a call from New Iceland, where the people were desperate for a pastor. Séra Jón agreed to go. He was to be paid $600 in the first year, but received $284 the first year (1877) and $319 the next. This was a very difficult time. The settlers in New Iceland faced extreme poverty and then came the small pox epidemic. There were no roads, and little food at times. Frú Lára started a school in Gimli, working without pay and Séra Jón walked all over New Iceland, from Winnipeg Beach to Hecla Island, to serve the people the best he could.

During this time (1877–1880) he came to Winnipeg several times each year and held services and performed pastoral acts. In 1880 Séra Jón went back to Iceland and served as a parish pastor in Seyðisfjörður, which was a small fishing village on the east coast of Iceland.

Séra Jón was very critical of the church in Iceland and impatient with the unwillingness of the church authorities to make any innovations to stengthen congregational life. I think this contributed to his decision to come back to Canada. He was also aware of the great need for ministers among the immigrants.

After Séra Jón came back in 1884, First Lutheran Church rapidly gained strength. Though not always in good health, Séra Jón was a hard and relentless worker. He was the president of the Icelandic Synod from its founding in 1885 until 1909, and the editor of the Synodical Monthly the *Sameiningin* from 1885 until 1913. He worked tirelessly for the strengthening of Christian education through Sunday Schools and through his efforts in establishing an Icelandic School, the Jón Bjanason Academy, which was located on Home St. just south of Sargent Ave. in Winnipeg.

As I read about Séra Jón, he emerges as an unusually gifted man, well educated and of a firm and at times unbending character. Those who were close to him adored him, while others saw him as being quite stern and manipulative. He was a good writer and expressed his opinions with great linguistic skill and sharp reasoning. Many felt that he could be far too scathing and self-assured as he went about taking his opponents to task.

Séra Jón did not hesitate to speak against anything or anyone who, in his opinion, worked against that which he saw to be for the good of the people. He fought against alchoholism and for the temperance movement. He wrote harshly about the church in Iceland for tolerating ministers who were drunkards, neglecting their duties and those who remained in the ministry even after they had abandoned their faith. I think it can be said that he was at times a thorn in the side of the church authorities in Iceland.

In his early days Séra Jón fought against his friend Séra Páll Thorláksson and the conservative influences of the Norwegian Synod. Rev. Friðrik Bergmann started out as a young man to the right of Séra Jón theologically, but as Bergmann leaned more and more towards the liberal theology and the humanism emanating from German theological school at the turn of the century, then Séra Jón found himself opposing him. He fought hard against unitarianism, which rejected the divinity of Christ.

Séra Jón was very consistent in his theology all his life. He saw scripture and the creeds as the basis for the Christian faith, he respected the Lutheran confessions, though he refused to give them the same status as the creeds. He was flexible, when it came to things that he considered of secondary inportance, such as in liturgical forms and whether a pastor should wear vestments or not, but very inflexible when it came to such things as the authority of the Bible, and some of the very basic teachings on the church. In such matter Séra Jón would give no quarter.

Séra Jón died at his home here in Winnipeg on July 3, 1914, 69 years of age. He is buried in Brookside cemetery and the words on the gravestone read: "He fought the good fight, he preserved the faith." (Paraphrasing II.Tim.4:7).

He was one of the bravest soldiers of Christ in the thousand-year history of the Christian Church among the Icelandic people.

Gimli Church Choir in bobsleigh to Hnausa Church.

Hálfdán Sigmundsson, Mail Carrier

"It was in October 1882 that at the request of Friðjón Friðriksson, I undertook to look after the transportation of mail from the Icelandic River to Clandeboye. I was to receive 35 dollars for the four winter months, eight dollars for each trip, but 12 dollars for each fall or spring trip. I felt then that this was a large sum of money, although to earn it I had to run 120 miles to make the round trip. But at the time I found walking easy.

"The community was sparsely settled and the main road generally impassable in winter. So I had to go from Sandy Bar along the lake to Gimli, often facing a strong wind, snow, and biting frost. I had to go two trips a month, and the trip usually took three or four days. Occasionally I made it in two days in March and April, if the weather was good and the road firm. I was seldom tired, for I found running easy, though conditions were often difficult for me.

"There were four homes along the way that provided food and lodging for the night, and were always ready to receive me, and treat me as if I were in the home of my own parents. The first was Stefán Sigurðsson's house on Drunken Point; the next that of the brothers Jóhannes and Guðlaugur Magnússon at Dagverðarnes in the Árnes community. The others were the homes of Pétur Pálsson at Gimli and Benedikt Arason at Kjalvík. These noble, charitable homes did everything for me that they possibly could without any recompense from me, but I know that God will reward every man who does kind deeds, at the time that He chooses.

"It was in January of 1883 that I left the Icelandic River with the mail at dawn, going towards Sandy Bar. At that time there was a storm from the south with snow and extreme frost. I went along the lake, intending to head south toward the Drunken River, and succeeded in doing so. Yet I never saw land till I had come close to the north side of the point. Then I went along the shore till I reached the home of my friend Stefán Sigurðsson, where I had food and coffee. At one o'clock I was ready to set out again on the lake. Stefán then told me that it was sheer madness for me to proceed along the lake in such wicked weather. I said that this was probably true, but that it was my belief that God would give me strength to overcome all my difficulties, and that this was not so much more difficult for me than than it was for my beloved wife at home to take care of the cattle and keep the house warm and look after the children. Then I took leave of him, saying that I hoped to see him again on the return trip.

"So I went on my way, not expecting to come to any dwelling till at Gimli. The weather was the same as when I left Sandy Bar. I often had turn my back to the storm to thaw the ice from my eyes and mouth with my bare hands. Off and on I glimpsed the shore while there was still daylight, and by dark I must have been east of Birch Point, north of Gimli. By then I was so exhausted and my clothes were so frozen that I found it difficult to walk, for I had perspired freely while I was still untired. Now I fully realized that it was doubtful that I would come out of it alive. Darkness had come, with blinding snow. Then I turned toward shore in the hope that the direction of the wind was still the same as it had been during the day, and

I thought then that I was east of Gimli. When I had walked approximately 15 minutes, I sank down exhausted and felt that it was impossible to rise again. I recited a prayer that my dear mother had taught me as a little boy. I lay there for a while and felt as though I had fallen asleep. Then I felt that I heard someone call to me, See the light! Whether I dreamed that someone called to me, I do not know, but it is certain that this voice, whether it came to me awake or asleep, saved my life. I rose and felt rested. The snowfall did not seem as heavy, and I glimpsed the woods. Now I beat my trousers at the knees with clenched fists to make walking easier. I had not begun to shiver, but felt extremely cold.

"When I had walked on for a little while, I saw directly ahead of me a flash of light resembling the light of a lantern. Now I walked on with all the speed I could muster, till with God's help I reached the home of my friend Pétur Pálsson. Then I beat upon the storm door, whereupon the master of the house came out and bade me welcome, and told me to hurry in out of this foul weather. I did so, and asked for water to drink, which I received, but was cautioned to drink it moderately. After slaking my thirst, I felt refreshed. Then Pétur's wife came and helped me to take off my frozen outer garments. When they drew the watch from my pocket, they felt that it was more like a lump of ice than a watch. I was dressed in warm clothing and put into bed with warm covers, and this excellent couple did everything in their power to nurse me. I fell asleep, after reciting the evening prayers that I had learned in childhood. The next day on waking I felt remarkably well. I reached Clandeboye that day, and the next day on the return trip the home of my friend Benedikt Arason in Kjalvík, and then arrived home the day after that.

"The recollection of the joy that I felt when from out on Lake Winnipeg I saw on shore the light that guided me to human habitation is always precious to me. Yet it is still dearer to me to recall how well my wife received me when I came home. During our time together the light of her love has lit the way for my soul and will do so till the end of life."

SIMON SIMONSON

Between Christmas and the New Year we carried dry wood out on the lake, to build a huge pyre for the burning out of the Old Year. On New Year's Eve the night was still and extremely frosty. The fire was lit and as soon as the blaze gave sufficient warmth, men and women, as many as were able to, thronged on the scene. Everybody enjoyed himself greatly. William Taylor, who was then about sixty years of age, was dressed to impersonate the Old Year. He was a sight to behold in his apparel. He wore a tar-paper hat, two feet high or better, a beard of hair of rabbit fur, and a white smock so voluminous as to make him seem a giant. He had a walking stick and carried a bottle and a wine glass. The latter he passed around freely, but there was a rub: the bottle was empty. He was very witty and his entertainment was good. Finally he was carried away and disappeared from the story. Then the twelve New Year's sprites appeared on the scene, clad in white and decked with rose-red ribbons. They acted in their various comic scenes. Then the people returned to their homes. thinking the entertainment a success. None had far to go, and there was plenty of wood for heating the shacks, which was all to the good, for the frost was very severe.

—from "The Reminiscences of Simon Simonson," trans. William Kristjánson, *The Icelandic Canadian,* Winter, 1946.

1920s, "Lady of the Lake" and "Amisk," Gimli.

A Few Words about the Icelandic Settlement in Minnesota

Snorri Högnason
Minnesota, January 25, 1878

The Icelandic settlement in Minnesota is situated in the northwestern part of Lyon County and the southern part of Yellow Medicine County. Comprising an area of 12 square miles, it is 76 miles north of the boundary between Iowa and Minnesota, and 24 miles east of the Dakota–Minnesota boundary, 300 miles south of the border between Minnesota and Manitoba, or from 44° 48" to 50° north latitude and between 95° 58" and 96° west longitude.

The closest trading centre for the Icelanders is called Nordland, a new little community, but very lively, which looks as though it will have a good future. It is on the Winona and St. Peter Railroad, about 5 miles southwest of the settlement. The land in and around the settlement is a grassy plain of ancient formation, with rounded hills, more or less stony, here and there. The soil is very fertile and well suited for the cultivation of crops, especially wheat, which grows very well here, producing 20–30 bushels to the acre and even up to 40 bushels. Pasturage for livestock is good on these plains and the hay crop the best. In some places the grass is four to five feet high and it is easy for one man, using a scythe with a long handle, to mow sufficient winter fodder for one cow in a single day. There are no forested tracts worth mentioning closer than 16 to 20 miles from the settlement. A great deal of government land in the neighbouring districts has not yet been applied for, but it is being taken up rapidly, and it is therefore most advisable for anyone interested in coming here to obtain land to come as early as possible in the spring.

There are three ways in which government land may be acquired here: one can obtain 160 acres by paying 2 dollars and 50 cents for the claim (papers) one makes when he settles on the land, then after residing there for six months or within a period of two and a half years, he is supposed to pay 400 dollars if the land lies within the area served by a railway, but only 200 dollars if it is outside that area.

Otherwise, one can take up 80 acres inside or 160 acres outside the railway area by paying 14 dollars for the papers to be taken out when he settles on the land, and then live there for five years, with absences of no longer than 6 months duration. At the end of five years he can obtain title to the land, but has first to pay the taxes on it.

In the third place, one can acquire 160 acres by paying 16 dollars when the land is taken up, having within four years planted 40 acres with trees, and obtaining full title after eight years if the forested area has begun to thrive. This applies only to unforested land. One is not required to reside on these lands any longer than he deems necessary. Livestock is valued here at the following rates: one cow, 20–25 dollars; one ox for ploughing, 100–120 dollars; ewes, 3–5 dollars; 2 horses, 150–300 dollars. Food prices: 1 bushel of wheat, 80–90 cents; 1 bushel of potatoes, 50–75 cents; beef, 3–5 cents a pound; sugar, 12½–16½ cents a pound.

The first group of Icelanders came to Lyon County in Minnesota late in June of 1875; they were six altogether, one family and a single bachelor. The father of the family, Gunnlaugur Pétursson from Hákonarstaðir in Jökuldalur, took up land, 160 acres, began by building a rough cabin for himself and later in the summer ploughed three acres.

Now he has 25 acres under cultivation and 21 head of cattle. These people came from Wisconsin, where they had been living for nearly two years.

The next to come arrived here in June, 1876, three families and two unattached men, eighteen in all. These people also came from Wisconsin. The heads of families took up land at once close to the first Icelander who had settled here. In the course of the summer they ploughed 12 acres, and two of them built cabins, but one did not build on his land until last spring. Later in the summer three families arrived here from Iceland, nine people, as well as a bachelor from Wisconsin. In 1877 forty-nine Icelanders came to the settlement; most of them came from Iceland late in the summer of 1877, the others from Wisconsin and eastern Minnesota.

All told, there must be 85 Icelanders here, including several single men who have taken jobs outside the settlement. Eleven Icelanders have taken up from 160 to 180 acres of land, nine have built houses for themselves, three of which are partially under ground level, the other six of timber, all of which were erected last summer, and a seventh under construction now. One of these is a log cabin, but the others are constructed of sawn boards in the American style.

Most of these houses are well built and some of them probably cost over five hundred dollars. The Icelanders here have 93 acres of ploughed land, divided among nine men. They have 85 head of cattle, divided among fourteen owners. Of these, eight are teams of oxen. In addition, they have pigs and a large amount of poultry. The Icelanders have enjoyed excellent health since coming here, as evidenced by the fact that only one individual has died, an elderly woman named Þórunn from Tókastaðir in Eyðaþinghá, who came here last summer after suffering for a long time from consumption.

Of church and school matters here there is little to report. The Icelanders have been without pastoral services since they came here, except for Pastor Páll Thorláksson coming on the 7th of last October to help men organize an Icelandic Lutheran congregation, on which occasion he conducted services on two farms, on October 7th and 8th. On the latter date he called a meeting at which he asked the men to vote on the provisional congregational by-laws he had prepared for their consideration. But some of them regarded several articles as being too restrictive and therefore unacceptable, so nothing came of organizing a congregation at the time.

Since then no action has been taken with respect to church matters, although most of the people would like to have an Icelandic minister if they can find one to their liking. Children born in the settlement have been baptized by Norwegian pastors here in the vicinity.

On the 19th of this month the Icelanders here held a meeting to discuss the opening of a school; it was decided to have a winter term of six weeks, provided enough money can be collected to pay the salary of a teacher. Whether anything comes of this remains to be seen, but we shall report on later developments.

Vínarterta

Vínarterta is a Viennese torte that was popular first in Denmark, then in Iceland in the 1860s and 70s. The fad soon ended in Iceland, but the immigrants who came to Canada continued to make it. It is the national dish of New Icelanders, though it is rarely seen in Iceland itself.

To make:
Cream 1 cup of butter well. Add 1½ cups sugar gradually. Add 3 eggs, one at a time. Beat after each addition. Add 1 teaspoon almond extract, 1 cup light cream. Add 4 cups sifted all-purpose flour with 3 teaspoons baking powder and ¼ teaspoon salt. Work in the flour as much as possible. Turn out on a pastry board. Divide into seven equal parts, roll thin and bake in a rather quick oven. Spread the following prune filling between layers.

Prune filling:
Soak ½ cup pitted prunes and cook until tender. Add 2½ cups sugar and bring to a boil. Cook until tender. Remove from stove and add 1 tablespoon vanilla and 1 teaspoon crushed cardamom. Let filling cool before spreading between layers. Ice with thin butter icing with almond flavour. There is some dispute as to whether the authentic recipe calls for six layers or seven. We belong to the group of seven, but acknowledge that there may be some virtue to six.

Canada 1978

I

On soft nights, fish, silvered with moonlight
Slip into purple shallows.
The Icelanders, their tow rope cut,
Drifted into this same bay.
A hundred years distant, their fears
And hopes have been reduced to death
And sepia photographs. Yet, during my dreams,
Their ordeal persists. Shod with bark
Slippers, their fingers rigid with frost,
They brave the future.
In 1876, dying with smallpox,
They sing hymns to an impatient God.

II

Somewhere, beyond Ile des Chênes,
Two half brothers
Slump sullenly beside a cold stove.
Each, jealous of a divided inheritance,
Waits suspiciously.

III

Everything has been destroyed.
The trees have been eroded by wind,
The tall grass has succumbed to snow,

IV

At midnight, a bottle of home brew
Clutched in my hand, I stop
At a pioneer graveyard. The stones
Sink beneath the earth.
I stumble among heavy spruce.
Behind me, the abandoned church
Is pale as old bone.
As the horned moon is engulfed by cloud,
Canada is plunged into darkness.

—W.D. Valgardson

1910, Old hull of steamer and sailboats at Gimli.

The Sunfish

David Arnason

Dawn was just spreading its red glow across Lake Winnipeg when Gusti Oddson reached for the buoy to pull in the first of his seven nets. And what was he thinking, that second cousin once removed of my great-grandmother, on a June morning in 1878? Perhaps he was thinking of the smallpox epidemic that had recently taken his wife and three children, or perhaps he was thinking about nets and why they sometimes caught fish and sometimes didn't. He wasn't thinking about talking fish, or at least the scattered diaries he left behind him give no indication that he was thinking about talking fish, and why, after all, should he have been? That's why he was startled when the sunfish he had just pulled into his boat, the first sunfish of the day, spoke to him.

"Gusti," the sunfish said, its silver scales bright in the first rays of the rising sun, "listen to me. I have much to tell you."

Gusti did not answer right away. He was a man of common sense, and he knew that fish do not speak. Still, in the past three years, his faith in common sense had been somewhat shaken. Common sense worked perfectly well in Iceland, but it seemed to be of less value in this new country. Common sense had told him that when water is covered with ice, you do not bother to fish. Here though, you fished underneath the ice, and when you pulled fish up through the ice, they gasped and froze solid in the winter air. Common sense told you that land which could grow trees fifty feet high could also grow potatoes, but that was apparently not necessarily so.

He had come to the Republic of New Iceland three years ago. The first year, he had nearly starved. The second year, his family had died in the smallpox epidemic. The third year, religious argument had split New Iceland into two warring camps. Seri Páll argued that the struggle between God and the devil was being fought out for the final time on the shores of Lake Winnipeg. Seri Jon argued that there was no devil, that Jesus was not the son of God, but only a religious leader, and that God was a spirit that was in everything in the world, but was not a person.

So, when the sunfish spoke to him, Gusti asked it, "Are you of the devil's party?"

"Don't talk nonsense," replied the sunfish, "there is no devil, or God either, for that matter,"

Gusti pondered for a moment, then asked, "Are you then a Unitarian?"

"I am a sunfish," said the sunfish, "and I'm not here to give you any selfish wishes. Greed and lust," he went on sadly, "that's all you find nowadays."

"Then you are one of the Huldafolk," Gusti said, "or maybe a Mori raised by enemies to bring me bad luck."

"More nonsense," the fish replied. "Ignorant superstition. How could your luck be any worse than it is? Everybody you love is dead. You haven't got a penny to your name. You hardly catch enough fish to eat, much less sell. Everybody in New Iceland calls you Gusti Foulfart because you live on dried beans and never wash your clothes. No woman will look at you."

"There is no need," Gusti told the fish, "to be rude. Things have not gone well for me in the last while, it is true, but that is not to say that they will not soon improve."

"Progress," sneered the fish, if indeed his opening and closing his mouth could be counted a sneer, "delusion, a snare and a trap, the vast enslaving device of the western world. Only peasants and fishermen and fools believe in progress. Things never get better, they only get different."

"How is it that you speak Icelandic?" Gusti asked the

fish, who seemed to be having some trouble with his breathing.

"A better question might be, 'How is it that you come to speak Sunfish?'" the fish replied, flopping around on the bottom of the skiff, as if to get a better view of Gusti. "Or indeed, it might to more to the point to ask, 'What is the nature of language?'"

"There are plenty of preachers on land," Gusti told the fish. "Already the sun is well above the horizon, and I have seven nets to lift. In New Iceland they have taken to calling me Gusti Madman because my wife sometimes comes to me in dreams and I cry out for her. I have no time to argue religion with a fish."

"Wait," cried the fish, with what might have been real fear, "I am speaking to you. Is this not remarkable? Do you not want to know what I have come to tell you?"

"I believe the evidence of my senses," Gusti replied, "when my senses give me evidence I can trust. I know that fish do not speak. Perhaps there is a voice-thrower on the shore, or perhaps I am still in my bed dreaming of fish. The least likely thing is that I am actually in my skiff talking with a fish. So, I am going to hit you on the head with my oar, and I will take you in and boil you and eat you with potatoes and butter. You are not a large fish, but you will do."

"Wait," the fish almost shouted, alarmed that Gusti had picked up an oar and seemed to mean business. Gusti had let go of the line and they were drifting away from the net toward the south-east. "I'll give you a wish. Not three wishes, but just one, and try to be reasonable."

Gusti put the oar down. "I'll have my wife back."

The fish groaned, or made a sound that was close to a groan. "I asked you to be reasonable. Your wife has been dead two years. How could you explain her return? Bringing people back from the dead destroys the natural order of things. Besides, you fought like cats and dogs when she was alive. Let me give you a new boat instead."

Gusti reached for the oar again.

"No, wait," the fish continued. "I can give you Valdi Thorson's wife, Vigdis Thorarinsdottir, instead. She's the most beautiful woman in New Iceland and you know you've lusted for her for years, even when your wife was alive."

Gusti pondered for a moment then replied, "No. She is a fine woman, but a man shall cleave to his wife. It is either my wife that you give me, or I eat you for supper this very night."

"Okay," the fish grumbled, "but it's not the way you think. She won't be waiting for you when you get back. She'll arrive in two weeks as a young woman, the cousin of your wife. Her name will be Freya Gudmundsdottir and she'll claim kin and come to live with you. But you'll have to woo her. And you'll have to shape up or else she'll marry Ketil Hallgrimsson, and then you'll have neither wife nor supper."

"Good," said Gusti, "that's fair. Now what have you come to tell me?"

The fish appeared to be sulking. "It's ridiculous," he complained. "I appear at great personal risk to offer mankind wisdom, and I get petty arguments, greed and lust. It's always the same. Do you think I like to breathe air? Do you think it's comfortable here on the bottom of this boat? I don't know why I do it."

The sunfish fell silent. Gusti felt a little sorry for it and he asked gently, "What is it I should know? I will listen carefully, and if things work out as you say and my wife returns, I will try to carry out your instructions."

The fish seemed a little mollified at this. "Okay," he said, "listen carefully."

Gusti leaned forward, attentive. "It's over," the fish told him. "Done. Finished. Kaput. They're closing down the whole show. Moving on to bigger and better things. They're closing down the whole show."

"What do you mean?" Gusti asked the fish, who by now was slowly opening and closing his mouth.

"All of it. Everything. Sun, moon, stars, trees, birds, animals, men, dogs, cats, the whole shooting works."

"You are telling me then," said Gusti, "that the world is going to end."

"You got it," said the fish, "go to the head of the class." He flopped once and continued, "And not a moment too soon."

"And when is this going to happen?" Gusti asked.

"I don't know. Maybe tomorrow, maybe a couple of millennia. They're busy, they've got things to do. Anyway, I've done my part. I've delivered the message. Now if you'll just heave me over the side, I'll be on my way."

Gusti ignored the fish. "This," he said, "is no great news. Everyone knows that the world will end some day. What matters is to live a proper life while you are here."

"Makes no difference," said the fish. "Proper or improper. What one man does is of no concern. If the whole world changed then maybe they'd reconsider. But it's far too late for that. And if you don't get me in the water soon, you're going to have my death on your conscience as well."

The fish's eyes had started to cloud over. "Just one last question," Gusti went on. "What day will my wife arrive?"

"You see," said the fish, as if addressing someone not in the boat but in the sky overhead, "you see what I have to put up with. I bring the most important message in the history of the universe and I have to answer foolish questions. Friday. Or Wednesday, or maybe Saturday. A week or a month. I've given you your wish. I'm not in charge of travel arrangements."

The fish had ceased to gasp, and lay in the bottom of the boat like a dead fish. Gusti picked it up gently, and slipped it into the water. The fish lay on its side, drifting slowly away from the boat. Gusti watched it for a long time, until finally, with a flick of its tail, it disappeared under the shining surface of the lake.

The next morning Gusti did not go out to his nets. Instead, he hauled water from the lake and heated it over an open fire. He took every article out of his shack and washed it. Then he washed the entire shack, inside and out, including the roof. He rechinked every crack he could

find with clay, and then he whitewashed the shack inside and out. The entire community came out to watch him with wonder. The children began by singing the song they always sang when he came near, "Gusti Foulfart, Gusti Foulfart, smells like rotten meat. Stinky beans and stinky fish is all that he will eat." Their parents hushed them and threatened to send them home unless they stopped.

Vigdis Thorarinsdottir was the only one brave enough to speak to him. She knew she was the most beautiful woman in New Iceland and she had seen Gusti look at her out of the corner of his eye.

"Gusti," she asked, "what happened? Are you expecting someone?"

"There has been a change," he replied. "The world will end soon and so a man cannot mourn forever. I will fish no longer. From now on I will be Gusti Carpenter. If you will make two blankets of the finest wool, I will repair the leaking roof on your shack which your husband will not repair because he prefers to sit on the dock repairing nets and telling stories. And, Alda Baldvinsdottir," he went on, "you have a cow. If you will give me a jug of milk each day for a year, I will put another room on your shack so that the twins will not have to sleep in the same bed with you and your husband, and you will not have to worry that he will roll over and smother them."

In this way, Gusti conducted business with the entire community. Halli Valgardson exchanged a year's supply of firewood for a new boat. Inga Gislasdottir agreed to make him a new suit in exchange for a brick chimney. The fishermen agreed to provide him with all the fish he could eat if he kept the dock in good repair. When the sun went down that day, Gusti was the richest man in New Iceland, and everyone had forgotten to call him Gusti Foulfart or even Gusti Madman.

One month later, twenty new settler arrived on Hannes Kristjanson's boat. They told frightening stories of the trip, how their ship had nearly foundered on the rocks on the coast of Scotland, and how a marvellous silver fish had appeared and led the boat to safety; how, coming up the St. Lawrence, they would surely have crashed into another ship had not a marvellous silver fish come to the Captain in a dream and warned him in time. Just that morning, coming down the Red River, they had run aground in the delta, but a school of silver fish had bumped into the boat until it floated free.

Among the passengers was Freya Gudmundsdottir. She was eighteen years old, with blond hair that hung down to her waist and eyes so blue that from that day on, no one in New Iceland called anything blue without explaining that it was not as blue as Freya's eyes. She looked like Gusti's wife had looked when she was young, but Gusti's wife had only looked pretty, and Freya was beautiful.

Ketil Hallgrimson was the first to meet her when she got off the boat. He asked her to marry him then and there, and he vowed to devote his life to making her happy. Ketil was a handsome young man, only twenty-three years old, with hair that hung in curls and muscles that rippled when he moved. The smile with which Freya answered him made Gusti's blood freeze. Still, she said she had not come to marry the first man she met, and she asked for Gusti. She told him she was the orphaned cousin of his wife, and asked if she might live with him until she could support herself. Gusti's tongue was so tied in knots that he could barely stammer yes.

She gave him her trunk to carry and followed him down the street to his newly whitewashed shack. The first thing she said when she got into the shack was, "I can see there hasn't been a woman's hand around here for a while." Then she scrubbed the table that Gusti had scrubbed until the top was thin. She sniffed the blankets that Vigdis Thorarinsdottir had just made and which had never been used. She screwed up her nose and hung them out on a tree to air. Then she swept the cleanest floor in New Iceland, threw out the fish that had been caught that morning, saying they had gone bad, and she started to make bread. Gusti sighed and thought, "Yes, this is my

wife all right. The fish has delivered his part of the bargain."

And that was pretty much the way things went until the following spring. Gusti found himself occupying a smaller and smaller part of the house. He left early in the morning to do the jobs he had promised the others, and he came back late at night to find the house getting cleaner and cleaner. Freya made him new clothes. She cut his hair and clipped his fingernails and toenails. He had almost no time to write in his diary, but what he wrote pretty well describes his life. "Thursday, January 11. Worked all day repairing Helgi's roof. I may no more chew tobacco." Any entry reads like any other.

Then that spring, Freya was chosen to be protector of the god in the wagon. Gusti should have expected it. Each year the prettiest young woman in the community was chosen, and Freya was certainly the prettiest of the young women.

Things changed very quickly. One morning Gusti awoke to find that his breakfast had not been made and Freya was not in her bed. He thought, because it was spring, that she might have gone for a walk, but she was not on the beach, nor was she in the garden behind the house. He walked to the dock and asked the fishermen if she had gone by. They laughed and said it would be some time before he saw her. He asked the children on the road, but they only laughed and ran away. Finally, he knocked on the door of Vigdis Thorarinsdottir, and she told him not to be a fool. "When the god in the wagon comes you will see her," Vigdis said, " now go away and act like a man."

Gusti knew then that he was in trouble. The protector of the god must marry that spring, and Gusti had not begun his wooing. Though they had shared the house for eight months, they were no closer than the day she had arrived. Gusti had been silenced by her wonderful beauty and even more silenced by her terrible temper. Still, he had changed for her. He was clean, obedient, sober and hard-working, an ideal husband. Ketil Hallgrimsson, on the other hand, had given up all work, and did nothing but sulk on the dock and wait till Freya came by, when he would leap to his feet and do tricks of strength until she had passed.

It was time, Gusti thought, to consult the fish. He walked all the way out to the south point and around to the channel, where the water was deep and he knew that fish like to sun themselves. He stopped near a large white rock and shouted to the gentle waves that lapped at the shore. "Sunfish, come out of the water, I have to talk to you," The only reply was the splash of a tern diving for minnows. He shouted again but still there was nothing but the quarrelling of gulls. He was about to leave, when he decided, "No, I have walked all this way, I will try once more. Sunfish," he cried, "come out." With a splash, the sunfish landed at his feet.

"If you would read something besides the newspaper," the sunfish said, "you would know that you have to call three times. Now what's wrong? Is the wife I brought you not good enough?"

"Oh, she's fine," Gusti replied, "even more beautiful than I remembered, though her temper is strong."

"You just forget," the fish said. "She is exactly as she was. You were just younger and didn't pay as much attention to her."

"Well," said Gusti, "she has not been chosen as protector of the god in the wagon, and so must marry this spring. What shall I do?"

"Marry her."

"I am not so sure she will marry me."

"Well, that's your problem, isn't it?" said the sunfish. "I've fulfilled my part of the bargain. Face it, you're getting on, you're not a young man anymore. And besides, you've become incredibly dull. You've given up tobacco, you don't drink, you work hard all the time, you've even shaved off your beard. What woman would give you a second glance?"

"There is no need to be insulting," said Gusti. "I have only asked you politely for advice."

"I'm busy," said the fish. "The world is coming to an end. I've got things to do. I have no time to give advice to the love-lorn." With a flick of his tail, he flipped himself back into the lake. Then his head appeared, silver in the sunlight, and he added, "Give her a magic philtre," and disappeared.

"What kind of magic philtre?" Gusti shouted at the waves, but the sunfish was gone and the waves didn't answer.

For the rest of the week, Gusti stayed in his house, watching the dishes go dirty, the dust begin to gather on the table and the floor. He stopped shaving and began to chew tobacco, spitting the juice into a basin on the floor. Freya did not appear. She was gone wherever the women had taken her to prepare, and he knew there was no reason to expect her. Once, Ketil Hallgrimsson came over and they shared a bottle, but neither had anything to say. In the community, women were frantically baking, and the men were decorating the doors with willow boughs. The first green leaves were starting to sprout on the poplars and maples, and already in some yards, the poppies were starting to bloom, white and yellow and red.

On Friday at dawn, she arrived. The whole community, men, women and children, had gathered in the street to await her. She came down the road from the south, dressed in a flowing white robe, her long golden hair ruffling in a slight breeze, her blue eyes flashing. Gusti thought he had never seen anything so beautiful. She was leading Helgi Gudmundson's white ox. The ox had a garland of flowers around its neck and was pulling the wagon with the god. The god was the largest Gusti had ever seen. He towered above the wagon and swayed with every step of the ox. His heavy hands, palms upturned for rain, rested on the front of the wagon. His shirt was a brilliant patchwork of colour and his great painted face beamed at the whole community. The wagon was filled with flowers and there were flowers and branches with green leaves sticking out of every crevice in the enormous body. Gusti noticed that one of the legs was draped in the blanket that Vigdis

Thorarinsdottir had made for him. "Where," he wondered, "where do the women find so many flowers, so early in the season?"

The ox stopped right at the foot of the dock, and Freya climbed into the wagon and seated herself in the lap of the god. She began the oration, and all the community sat down on the ground to listen. Gusti was so entranced by her beauty and her frailty, there in the lap of the god, that he hardly heard what she said. She spoke of rain. She spoke of sunlight and crops. She spoke of trees bursting out of the earth, of animals in the fields, of nets dripping with fish. She spoke of love and of little children. Her voice mingled with the voices of birds and the lapping of waves. And then she was gone.

Then the women brought out the steaming vats of coffee and plates full of pönnukökur. They brought out turkeys glazed with honey and chokecherries, chickens and pigeons and ducks. They brought out roasts of venison and roasts of beef, plates of boiled sunfish and fried pickerel and broiled whitefish. They brought out hangikjot and rullupylsa, lifrapylsa and slátur. They carried out bowls of skyr and ram's heads pickled in buttermilk. They brought out vinaterta and kleinur and ástarbolur.

The men pulled corks out of bottles and threw away the corks. They said, "It is never too early for good whiskey," and they aimed the bottoms of the bottles at the sun. The children were into everything, laughing and crying and squealing, but no one paid any attention to them. Husbands and wives who had hardly spoken for months kissed like young lovers, so it is no surprise that no one noticed that Gusti had slipped away and returned to his house.

Freya was there. She had changed from her white robe into an old blue housedress. She was staring out the window and hardly noticed Gusti's arrival. She seemed not even to have noticed the mess in the house. "You were wonderful," Gusti began. "Never has there been such a beautiful protector nor so clever an oration."

Freya glanced at him, then looked out the window once more. "I shall marry," she said. "In nine days, I shall marry."

"And who shall you marry?" Gusti asked, his heart wrenching inside him.

"There are many I might marry," Freya responded, though without enthusiasm. "In the meanwhile, it is not seemly that I should live longer with you. I will go to stay with Vigdis Thorarinsdottir until my wedding day." Then she packed her trunk, and Gusti carried it down the road to Vigdis's house.

The next day was quiet as the community rested from the celebration, but by Monday the town was buzzing with rumour. Who had Freya chosen? Would it be Ketil Hallgrimsson, or one of the other young men of the community? Or had she perhaps betrothed herself to an outsider who would arrive on the wedding day. There was even a rumour that the priest was angry because they had received the god in the wagon, and that he would refuse to perform the wedding ceremony. Ketil Hallgrimsson was dressed in his best clothes, and stood in the road before Vigdis Thorarinsdottir's house, doing feats of strength.

That week, Gusti had plenty of time to write in his diary. He pondered over what he might put in the philtre to gain Freya's love, and he wondered who might help him. He considered whether it was right to use a philtre at all. Could love that was gained by a trick be real? In the end, he decided that the philtre should contain pure water. What else, he thought, is so close to love? It may be taken cold or hot, it is clear and insubstantial, it refreshes, but when it is consumed it is gone. And most important, there is more of it in the world than anything else.

Here you must bear with me, because the diaries end, and so I have had to reconstruct what actually happened. My aunt Thora, whose mother was there, says that Gusti went to Vigdis Thorarinsdottir and told her of his trouble. She led him to a clearing in the bush where she comforted him in her own way and promised to slip the contents of the philtre into Freya's coffee on the morning of the wedding day. That morning, Freya chose Gusti and they were married and had thirteen children. Ketil Hallgrimsson was so sad that he drowned himself in the lake that same day.

My aunt Lara, Thora's sister, agrees with the story, but claims that Vigdis drank the water herself. That morning, Freya chose Ketil Hallgrimsson and he did not drown for twenty years. By that time, he had fathered all the children whose descendants now live in Arborg. Vigdis left her husband and went to live with Gusti and they had thirteen children, though they never married. All their descendants now live in Riverton.

The people from Arnes tell a story very much like the story of Gusti, but in their version, a marvellous stranger dressed all in silver appeared on a magnificent boat and claimed Freya for his bride. The moved to Wynard and had thirteen children and all the Icelanders in Saskatchewan are descended from them.

My cousin Villi, who is only six years older than me, but who speaks better Icelandic, says that the family is trying to hide something. He has overheard whispers, and he believes that Freya chose both Gusti and Ketil, that the three of them raised thirteen children and no one ever knew who was the father. He says the whole thing about the fish is just made up so people will think it is only a fairy tale and not enquire any further. After all, our uncle is the mayor, and any scandal might go bad for him in the next election.

I have my own ideas. If I were making up this story, I would tell you that, yes, Gusti did go to see Vigdis and tell her his troubles, and yes, she did comfort him in her own way, telling him of the secret love she had always felt for him and begging him to forget Freya. If it were my story, I could tell you that Gusti was not a flexible man, that he had made the faithful Vigdis pour the water into Freya's coffee, that she had chosen Gusti and they had married. Then, because I would want a happy ending, I would show

you how Freya's bad temper and wicked tongue drove Gusti away, so that he married the faithful Vigdis, while Freya chose the hapless Ketil, who, for all his feats of strength, could never get the better of her. I would say they each had thirteen children, and all the people of Gimli are descended from them.

But I would go even further, because a story needs a proper ending, and I would do something about the fish. I would let Gusti catch him once more in a net and when the fish began all that nonsense about the end of the world, I would have Gusti take him home to Vigdis, who would boil him and feed him to the thirteen children. So there you are.

GIMLI GIRLS

The girls of Gimli are dreaming,
wrapped in their honey-blonde hair
beside their landlocked sea of a lake
dreaming of water, dreaming of sunlight,
their pillows bunched under their long,
honey-blonde waving hair, their white
feather quilts pounding in billows
above them, seagulls etched in the blue
of their winter dreams, the hot
honey-gold sand that stretches the length of their dreaming
 all the long late morning light
slanting through windows when they
open their lake-blue light-seeing eyes
in the tumble and thrash,
the storm of the bedclothes, cover and sheets,
tossed in the wake of their waking.

—David Arnason

Coming of Age Among the Urban Icelanders: A West End Youth

John S. Matthiasson

My earliest memory of the West End – a neighbourhood of Winnipeg, Manitoba which stretched along both sides of Sargent Avenue for about ten city blocks and was home to at least two generations of Icelandic-Canadians – is of sounds. They were the sounds to which I awakened each weekday morning when I was seven years old and living temporarily at my grandparents home on Ingersoll Street, a few doors from Wellington just about at the geographical center of the West End of that time. The roomy wooden house had been built by my grandfather or Afi, and in it he and my grandmother or Amma, had raised their own eight children. During the years of the Great Depression it had been home to relatives and fictional relatives from the rural Icelandic-Canadian communities looking for employment and, in the 1940s and 50s, to grandchildren attending university in the city. For a while in the forties, it was the residence of my widowed mother, my infant sister, and myself.

The sounds I heard each morning were of shod feet of horses, clapping and clattering slowly along the pavement, and the blows of hammers. The horses pulled the wagons of the delivery men who went up and down the streets each day delivering bread, milk and ice, and the hammers were struck by carpenters building new houses on the few vacant lots left in the neighbourhood and, in the process, destroying some of the playgrounds of its children.

My mother, the third child of immigrants from Iceland, was born on Toronto Street, which was pretty much in the middle of the West End then. When she was still a child, and the neighbourhood had shifted farther west and taken

over more prairie ground, the family moved to the house her father had built on Ingersoll. My mother had learned Icelandic at home, but also found it to be the language of the street and only acquired English when she began public school. She and her siblings attended Principal Sparling school when it was still on the very western edge of the neighbourhood and when Icelandic could be heard in the hallways, for most of the students and teachers were Icelandic.

As a young woman attending First Lutheran Church – one of the two Icelandic churches in the West End, the other being the Unitarian, and more about that later – she met a young pre-Med student from one of the Icelandic settlements in North Dakota. They were married, and moved to Wisconsin, where my father studied dentistry, then set up a practice in a small town in the same state. He died when I was seven years old, and my mother returned to the place of her childhood, with an infant daughter and a young son and paid the bills by teaching piano. We all stayed at the two-story house on Ingersoll for a few months before moving into a small bungalow on Lipton, the next street over.

My own earliest West End memories, then, are of sounds. Born a decade or so later, I might have been imprinted with the reverberations of automobiles, but there were few of them in the West End of the 1940s. Many of the men were away fighting a foreign war, and few women drove cars in those days. If my mother needed something from the department stores downtown, she took my sister and I along and we all walked the mile or so each way. If we were good, and didn't bother her while she shopped, she would buy us each a thick, creamy, chocolate malt in the basement of the Hudson's Bay Store on Portage and Vaughan. Downtown shopping was almost always done by West Enders in the stores along Portage. Main Street also had shops and larger stores all along it, but it was the provenance of North Enders, and alien territory to us. There was a separateness to the ethnic peoples of the city in those days, and they tended to stay away from one another's territories. The Icelanders always claimed that they were not ethnic, but the West End was an enclave as much as any of those in the North End, with its Jews, Ukrainians and others. It was just that the Icelanders were too snobbish to admit it.

The world I inhabited was more one of the back lanes than the front streets, for it was along those that we boys played games like kick-the-can with discarded tin cans we recovered from kitchen garbages. When girls were part of the gang, though, the sidewalks were where we played games of "mister, may I" and hide-and-seek. If there were no boys about, girls joined in hopscotch and simple rope skipping.

One thing is certain, and that is that our outdoors world was not populated by adults. In the evenings parents played bridge, worked on small garden plots or read books and magazines, but they did not seem concerned about making certain that our spare time was taken up with constructive learning activities, as do parents today. Their worlds and ours intersected in places, such as the dinner table, but mostly they were separate from one another. If we were enrolled in classes at the downtown YMCA or took music lessons we walked or rode our bicycles.

The West End had not been planned by suburban developers. Instead, houses were built by private contractors such as my Afi, and the first ones went up on street corners. This left, in the middle of most blocks, a few vacant lots, and these were claimed by the young. Sargent Park had its open, groomed, and spacious grounds, and school field days were held there. In winter, many of the lots were flooded, and became skating rinks. Boys would practise their hockey skills on them or join the team of one of the community clubs such as West End Memorials. The girls simply skated in circles under the eyes of their bashful male counterparts, the more brazen of whom would skate after them while more timid ones would stand on the sidelines and make salacious jokes with one another.

Beside most rinks stood one room shacks, the domain of the older men hired to take care of the rinks. They were always heated by potbelly stoves burning coal or wood. The man in charge would usually sit near the fire and sharpen skates. The shacks had a rich aroma of warm wood and heavy, wet, woolen clothing. Again, like the sounds, the scents of the West End stay with us. If skates needed refurbishing, or better sharpening than could be done at the local shack, they were taken to Jack, the Scottish shoemaker, whose tiny shop behind a small confectionery on Lipton and Wellington was always filled with the rich smell of leather. Jack's little hovel and the confectionary are gone now like so many of the West End landmarks.

In the summers both boys and girls gathered at the vacant lots in the evenings. We lit bonfires with scrap lumber from building sites and brush collected from the nearby prairie. Each person would throw a potato or two into the fire, and we would tell stories and, if they were brave enough, the older boys would do a little necking with the girls. As the fire died down to embers, the potatoes would be knocked out with a stick and reclaimed by their owners. We broke open the hard baked and blackened skins and passed around a salt shaker to spice up the hot white meat. Wieners and marshmallows were too expensive for most of us, but we could always find potatoes in our parents' basements. I have never since tasted a potato which compared with those cooked in a fire on a West End lot.

In time – and especially after the war ended and men returned home – houses were built in the vacant lots. In the evenings, after the workmen had left for their homes,

c. 1930, Kristin Benson (Kristofferson) and Humphrey Olson.
Photo from the collection of Kristin Kristofferson in
the archives of Terry Tergesen.

the half-built houses provided great play spaces for the young, until some resident, worried about accidents, would call the police or come to chase us away himself.

I almost forgot Sargent Park. The streets of the West End were far more fun than the manicured fields of the park, but its outdoor swimming pool held a special fascination in the heat of summer. It was always too crowded to swim on those days – and especially when Principal Sparling school was closed because of heat – but we enjoyed jumping in place in the water or lying on towels along the side soaking up sun and eyeing the other sex.

Another popular activity in summer for boys was crab apple raiding. Groups of us would scale fences and fill our pockets before the lights would go on and the owner came out to drive us off his property. The apples were too sour to eat, and we would throw them at one another as we walked down a lane. I seem to remember that most of the yards we raided were those of British or Scottish residents, but I don't think there was any ethnic prejudice which motivated us – it was just that the Icelanders didn't grow as many apple trees.

There were not many restaurants in Winnipeg in the forties and fifties, other than ones in Chinatown which specialized in Chinese cuisine, but every drugstore had a soda fountain. Milkshakes and malts were our favorites, but you could also purchase any one of a number of flavours of sodas, and if your budget didn't extend to buying something with ice cream in it, you could always buy a cherry coke. Jack St. John's drugstore on Lipton and Sargent was the busiest in the West End, and there was Harmon's drugstore up on Portage and Sherbrook, where you could also get a hamburger or hot dog. Harmon's was a few doors down from Bjarni's barber shop – a popular place for West End Icelanders to have their hair cut and catch up on neighbourhood gossip. Women tended to patronize Lil's Beauty Shop on Ellice and Arlington.

For more substantial fare, there were the fish and chips shops. The merchandise was wrapped in the British manner in layers of newspaper. We would douse the bag with vinegar and walk home or to an after-school job munching on the potatoes, regardless of how cold the weather might be.

In the homes of the Icelanders, Icelandic food would be prepared and offered to guests at Christmas, and in the main it consisted of different types of sausages, all made from mutton and served on the dark brown Icelandic molasses bread, along with the many-layered cake, vínarterta, which has been adopted by so many non-Icelanders. The thin Icelandic pancakes, or pönnukökur, were sprinkled with either brown or white sugar and rolled up tightly. My Amma had a cast iron griddle which she used only for making pancakes. She made them on a tiny stove which she kept in the basement of the house, and perhaps this small cooking area was a New World replacement for the summer kitchens of the Icelandic farmsteads. The smell of Amma's pancakes wafted up the stairs and spread through the house, but the stove in the cool basement didn't increase the temperature.

The Icelandic West Enders were known throughout Winnipeg for their coffee, and almost all of them made it in the old fashioned way by boiling water and then pouring it through a cotton bag suspended in the coffee pot. The non-Icelanders claimed that the bags were actually old socks, but they never turned down a cup of Icelandic coffee, and some even drank it the Icelandic way, by sipping it through a sugar lump held between the teeth.

The hallways of Principal Sparling elementary school were coated with distilled memories of a couple of generations of Icelandic pupils. But the time after school and on Saturdays was not always play time either. Some of us went to First Lutheran Church on Saturday mornings for Icelandic language lessons, but my own were private lessons from a friend of my mother. Unfortunately, few of us were able to master the language, and I am afraid that we had little incentive to do so, in spite of the hopes of our parents.

Whenever I returned home from school I had the tasks

of stoking the furnace in the basement with coal and bringing up potatoes and turnips from the large gunny sacks in which they were kept. The basement was clammy and damp, and the potatoes co-existed with small spiders, of which I was terrified. Many neighbourhood boys on long paper routes delivered the Free Press or Tribune which went from Notre Dame to Sargent or Sargent to Portage Avenue along the ribs of the neighbourhood – three long city blocks in either case. Later we might work setting pins in a downtown bowling alley. It was a tough and dirty way to earn spending money, and it was often dangerous, as flying pins could go in unpredictable directions. Or we might deliver for a drugstore. In those days every drugstore had delivery boys who worked in the evenings taking drugs to people who had called in prescriptions or soft drinks to those wanting refreshments. Winnipeg winters were not easy times to ride old fashioned bicycles weighted down with heavy baskets.

Disposable cash was especially important when "drapes" were the fashion in male clothing. These were individually designed pants, wide at the knee and tapered at the ankle, and they came in a variety of colors. Three, four and even five exposed seams decorated the sides and the pants rose up above the waist several button lengths, depending on how much the designer could afford. We designed our own, and tried to outdo one another in the process. Of course, drapes were tailor made, and expensive.

My own first job in the West End I inherited from my uncle Harold, who had done it twenty years before me. The job was as helper for Joe the Baker, whose horse-pulled bakery van was one of those which had awakened me when I was seven. Joe's real name was Tryggvi, but at least two generations of West Enders had known him as Joe. The story was that when he had first arrived from Iceland he had replaced another delivery man who had gone on vacation. When the regular driver returned, he discovered that Tryggvi had made all of the entries in the books in Icelandic. Tryggvi or Joe was kept on, as he was

SKYR

Commercially made skyr is now easily available in Manitoba. The skyr should be taken from the package, mixed with cream and sugar to taste, and beaten until smooth and of the consistency of soft ice cream. It is often eaten with fruit or with syrups or jellies.

To make:
Bring 4 cups of whole milk to a boil. Cool until lukewarm. Set aside ½ cup warm milk and add two tablespoons of skyr to it. Stir into the remaining milk. Add twelve drops of rennet, stir well, and store in a warm place for twenty-four hours. Drain liquid from curds through a piece of cheesecloth. What remains is skyr.

Cold skyr is sometimes mixed with cold oatmeal porridge (2 skyr to 1 oatmeal) and eaten with brown sugar and cream. This is called Hræringur. It is eaten mostly by the very old.

the only Icelandic employee of the bakery, and so the only person who could translate the entries, but told to begin doing it in English.

I would meet Joe every Saturday morning at the bakery on Alverstone and Portage and drive the horse while Joe sorted out the breads and cakes. During the day he would leave me alone on the rig while he went into unlocked houses for coffee. My Amma always left the pot on the stove for Joe, and it did not matter whether she or anyone else was home, for vandalism was virtually unknown in the West End of that time. While he was in the homes, I would sit behind the horse and fantasize that I was driving a covered wagon along the prairie trails behind Gene Autry or one of the other cowboy heroes my friends and I watched at the matinees at the Rose theatre. In the late afternoon we stopped at Jack St. John's drugstore for coffee for Joe and hot chocolate for me. I was paid fifty cents for the day.

Icelanders are voracious readers, and books were important to the Icelandic youth of the West End. Most of us collected comic books, which sold for a dime a piece, and periodically we would get together with friends to trade them.

The magazine rack in Jack St. John's served another purpose, for in those times there was no Playboy, but several sun-bathing magazines were sold. Sheepishly, young boys would sneak looks inside them, gaining their first images of the opposite sex from the photographs of female nudists. Young girls may have done the same thing, but I never asked them if they did, and they probably wouldn't have told me if I had.

There were two other playgrounds, both of them on the western fringe of the neighbourhood. One was the gravestone cutters on Erin or Wall, west of Sargent Park. In it, huge slabs of marble were tossed together in oddly shaped piles waiting to be taken out and cut down into markers for graves. We were warned to stay away but we ignored the warnings. Among the slabs were caves to be explored, and standing precariously on the tops of the piles

was like reaching the peak of a mountain for prairie children used to a flat landscape. The workmen would chase us away during the week, but on weekends we had the area to ourselves, and no man-made amusement park could compete with the enjoyment we gained from playing there.

The other was the city dump – a massive hill of refuse located south of Wellington Avenue. After the war ended, it was a place where we could retrieve army helmets and other discarded military paraphernalia. The dump itself, rising high over the flat terrain, was, like the marble slabs of the gravestone cutters, a place of geographical interest for prairie children, and we enjoyed romping among the refuse and discovering cast-off treasures. Today it is covered with grass and has been turned into a park, but I don't think anyone uses it.

Much of what I have described happened in other areas of the city as well, and there is nothing distinctively Icelandic about the activities. But, the children who engaged in them were the children or grandchildren of Icelandic immigrants, and lived in homes in which Icelandic coffee was made each morning and the Icelandic language was used by adults when they wanted to speak without being understood by the young. They had Icelandic surnames, even if many of both sexes had been given more generic personal names. I know that my own mother named me John because that was the name of one of my grandfathers, but also because, with its anglicized spelling, it did not have an ethnic ring. On Sundays they attended churches which still had Icelandic language services in the evenings. On the coffee tables in the living rooms of their homes or, more likely, on the kitchen tables, could be found copies of one or the other of the two Icelandic weekly newspapers printed in publishing houses located on Sargent Avenue, which was know to the rest of Winnipeg as Icelandic Main Street. My companions and I were growing up in a community which denied its ethnic nature, and yet was profoundly ethnic. The Icelanders of my mother's generation may have made an issue of learning to speak English without an Icelandic accent, but they did not lose the language itself or pride in an Icelandic identity. The West End was Icelandic to the core, and no one disputed it

West Enders did not meet discrimination when they ventured out of their own neighbourhood into the larger community. Instead, they seemed to be welcomed and even embraced by the dominant WASP population. Young Icelandic women were sought after as brides, and men who had graduated in law and medicine found little difficulty being accepted into established firms and prac-tices. Unfortunately at times the West Enders even took on the prejudices of the establishment.

Icelanders in Winnipeg and throughout the province were called "goolies," but it was not a pejorative term. Unlike ethnic labels such as "kike" and "hunkie," it was not a fighting word, and most Icelandic West Enders laughingly used it to describe themselves. The roots of the word goolie are lost in Manitoba history. David Arnason claims it is a Ukrainian expression used in the Interlake district of the province for Icelandic neighbours, but I prefer the urban, or West End, explanation, which is that

1950, commerical fishing in Gimli.

MOM'S ICELANDIC BREAD

To make:
Scald 2 cups of milk. Add 1 tablespoon melted butter, ½ cup brown sugar, 1 cup baking molasses and 1 teaspoon salt. Cool to lukewarm. Add 2 packages dry yeast to ¾ cup lukewarm water in which 2 teaspoons sugar have been dissolved. Let stand 10 minutes. Add to milk mixture and gradually add 4 cups white flour and 4 cups graham flour (or whole wheat), one cup at a time. Knead well. Let rise in warm place until double in bulk. Punch down and form again into loaves in buttered pans. Let rise again in pans until nearly double in bulk. Bake at 350° for 45 minutes. Yields 3 loaves.

The amount of molasses is a matter of taste, and varies according to how the bread will be used. Larger amounts (1 cup) are used if the bread will be used with rúllupylsa. Smaller amounts (¼ cup) for everyday use.

goolies are named for the old 'goolie hall' on Sargent Avenue. The goolie hall was originally the headquarters of the IOGT, or Icelandic Order of Good Templars. A fairly large building of several floors, it was for many decades the social center for Icelandic activities in Winnipeg. Dances were held there, as well as the famous debates which drew large crowds and fanned arguments in the community. In many ways, the goolie hall was a physical metaphor for the West End to outsiders.

Much of the folklore of the West End which we learned as children related to the goolie hall. It was the meeting place of one of the two temperance leagues the Icelandic immigrants formed to try and deal with the well-known Icelandic liking for strong spirits, but it was also much more than that. When I was growing up it stood on the inner-city edge of the neighbourhood, and the area around it had begun to deteriorate. Once standing in the hub of the West End, it had become isolated as the residents opened up new territory to the west. By the 1940s occasional dances and bingos were held there, but the temperance movement had expired and with it the old building had lost its identity.

In earlier times the hall was filled night after night with Icelanders drawn to the heated debates held in it. That was before movies and television provided sources of entertainment. The Icelandic community had always been a divided one - divided on virtually every issue. There were the conservatives and the liberals, represented in political affiliations and commitment to theologies. Everyone took one side or the other, with little attempt at compromise. In fact, the people loved the debates, which provided intellectual stimulation. In polite English society, politics and religion were unacceptable topics of conversation, but to Icelanders they provided necessary ingredients for good conversation. The factions – conservative and liberal – each had its own advocate in one or the other of the two Icelandic newspapers, *Lögberg* and *Heimskringla,* both published in the West End but serving the entire Icelandic network in North America. In religion, there were the two

forms of Lutheranism – conservative and New Theology – and then the upstart Unitarianism. The differences over religion were so marked that Lutheran parents strove to prevent their offspring from marrying Unitarians, and vice versa, although they were only partly successful.

Every position had its own leaders, and it was these men who would argue with one another in formal debates on the stage of the goolie hall. Their arguments gave the audiences ample material to ruminate on as they later sat in the Wevel Cafe drinking coffee through their sugar lumps. The public debates were a form of theatre and according to the folklore of the West End, the speakers would meet before their public appearances and walk the backlanes together planning their strategy. Then, at the goolie Hall they would stand up and denounce their opponents in the strongest language. I remember being told about a theological debate in which one of the two members put his arm out in a sweeping gesture and proclaimed to his antagonist, "Get thee behind me, Satan." And yet, apparently the two leaders respected one another, and met for their secret walks like professional wrestlers after a match. For them, friendship seemed to have little to do with intellectual disagreements, although the issues they kept alive with their rhetoric divided the community.

The Lutheran church on Victor just off Sargent and the Unitarian church on Banning and Sargent gave spiritual sustenance to the community for decades, as well as providing material for the debates, but in time both lost their Icelandic character. The Unitarian was taken over by university intellectuals in the 1960s and First Lutheran lost many of its younger members to St. Stephen's, built far to the west in a suburb constructed on what had earlier been open prairie. The Icelandic language is rarely, if ever, heard in the sanctuaries and meeting rooms of either today.

For many years, Icelandic educational needs were met at the Jön Bjarnason Academy, a private school in the West End supported by the Icelandic population of the province. Although it had been originally sponsored by Lutherans, its program was an accommodation to the Unitarian fact, and attracted pupils from both denominations. During its first years, Lutheran students were expected to attend mandatory classes in religious instruction, but others were given study hours instead. The doors of "the J.B.," as it was fondly known, were finally closed in 1940, after twenty-seven years, but it left an indelible mark on the Icelandic community of the entire province and beyond, for many had passed through its programs.

Today Betelstadur, a senior citizens' residence, stands on the what was for a long period the extreme western edge of the West End as well as the city of Winnipeg. Now the city extends for many miles farther out. Residents of this complex are almost all West Enders, and most of those are of Icelandic background. Icelandic can be heard in the lounge area and on the elevators, but the speakers are not young people, and they do not use it when talking with their children and grandchildren. The residence is the last bastion of the Icelandic community in the West End, a microcosm of what was once a definable community.

Fish flies were thick that summer.

From the Secret Diary of Svanhildur Sigurdson, Age 12

Lesley Peterson

for my aunt, Margaret Eggertson Munroe

Monday, November 6, 1950

Dear Diary,

We learned about Bonnie Prince Charlie in school today. I have decided to be a Jacobite. Too bad we don't live in the olden days. I asked Miss Miller if there was anybody nowadays who could be the rightful heir to a throne. She said not in the Interlake.

Miss Miller's first name is Anne. With an "e." Svanhildur is like Anne only it has a "-hildur" at the end instead of an "e." That's what comes of being born in Siglunes instead of in Winnipeg.

Baldy Jonasson dipped my braids in the inkwell again today. I called him a pig so he snorted. Then I called him a greedy bloodsucking Conservative fish buyer. He kept snorting. Miss Miller made us both apologize. When Baldy said sorry he had his fingers crossed.

Mom says I can order a new dress for Christmas. I wanted the pink one on page 18 but Elsie Eggertson says she's ordering that one. So I went to look for the Eaton's catalogue just before supper and Einar had it. He said he was looking at flannel shirts. David said he was looking at the ladies' underwear. Mom said she was almost finished knitting some new socks and that Einar could have them if he wanted. Dad sent them both outside to chop wood. Einar took the Eaton's catalogue with him.

If Auntie Frieda doesn't invite me to Winnipeg for Easter I think I will die.

P.S. Canned mutton for supper.

Tuesday, November 7, 1950

Dear Diary,

Uncle Jonas is here. It's 8:00 so they're all sitting in the kitchen rolling cigarettes and sucking coffee. I don't know how Miss Miller can stand it. She's read *Anne of Green Gables*. She knows better. Gilbert Blythe never pours his coffee into the saucer before he drinks it. Jack London never sticks sugar cubes between his teeth. I've read every book in the Siglunes School library. All ten of them. Even *Ivanhoe*. And Ivanhoe never sucks sugar cubes. So that just shows you, doesn't it?

Mom's after me again to practise reading my Icelandic. We go this big box of books from the Ericsons and we're supposed to pass them on to the Haldursons when we're done. She and Dad and Amma have read them all already. I keep telling them I have homework.

I hate Baldy Jonasson. Don't ask me why. I'm so mad I can't tell you.

P.S. Mutton again. Mom says maybe fruit preserves tomorrow. Big-nose Alex says he used to eat hay when he was a boy. He's only the hired man and I don't think I believe him.

Wednesday, November 8, 1950

Dear Diary,

Icelandic books never get it right. Take *Littla Gula Heinen,* for instance. *The Little Yellow Hen.* I actually used to like that book – back when I was a child. Before I found out that it's really supposed to be "the little *red* hen." You have to learn everything the hard way around here.

Uncle Jonas is mad at Cousin Sigga. He's going to Iceland to celebrate his 70th birthday and Cousin Sigga says she's going with him. Mom says he's an old goat and what's a man his age planning to do that his daughter couldn't know about. Dad says someone should remind him that it's Reykjavík he's going to and not Copenhagen. I asked Miss Miller what did Dad mean about Copenhagen and she just said I'd do Denmark next year in grade 8. Do they want me to get an education or not?

Mrs. Bjornson says I have to have "Country Gardens" hands together by tomorrow. I hate counting eighth notes. Auntie Frieda says if I pass my exam she'll take me to sneak preview night at the Uptown Theatre when I go to Winnipeg. I know I will never make it. If I don't fail my exam first I will probably die of an overdose of boiled mutton.

Amma is carding wool tonight. She always says Icelandic poetry out of her head while she does that. Poems and stories. I guess she likes them.

Maybe I did write "Hildy Sigurdson loves Bonny Prince Charlie" inside my history notebook a few times but Baldy Jonasson didn't have to show it to every boy in Siglunes. Besides, Elsie told me to do it.

Thursday, November 9. 1950

Dear Diary,

Another rotten day. Miss Miller told Dad that I was interested in Scottish history. So he pulled out that Bobby Burns book of his again and he made me sit there and listen. I will never clean her blackboards again. Dad read FIVE poems. Long ones. What kind of a name is Tam O'Shanter anyway? At least David and Einar had to listen too. I have decided not to be a Jacobite after all. I forgot they didn't really speak English.

Then Mrs. Bjornson rapped my knuckles. She said my "Country Garden" was more like a wilderness. Very funny.

Uncle Jonas was here again. He and Mom are making lists of all the people we're related to over here so that he can take them over to Iceland and bring back more lists from Iceland of all the people we're related to over there. Mom won't let Dad make the lists because if he doesn't like people he leaves them off.

Uncle Jonas says he's going to take his camera with him to Iceland. When he gets back I'll get to look at about a hundred pictures of rocks and small hairy ponies. Maybe he'll be really lucky and see a volcano erupt. Miss Miller says she doesn't think the Interlake will ever get a volcano. But she doesn't know everything.

We have a history test tomorrow. I can't study. I threw my notebook in the furnace.

P.S. Hardfish tonight. A change but not exactly a rest.

Friday, November 10, 1950

Deary Diary,

Poor Charlie. I feel so sorry for him and everyone else just thinks it's funny. Especially Big-nose Alex. Charlie followed Alex when he drove the hay wagon out to the field today. Charlie does that a lot – he's very friendly. Little did the hapless animal expect the terrible nightmare that this seemingly innocent afternoon held in store for him. (I thought that up during supper.)

On the way back from the field one of the tires blew on the wagon. Naturally Charlie thought he'd been shot. Charlie is a very sensitive pig. That poor, terrified creature squealed and took off for home and when he shot into the yard he was still squealing. Expecting to drop dead any second of course and only looking for a loving lap to die in. And now everybody's laughing at him. It's so cruel. Dad kept putting down his fork to say "gasping and snorting like the devil was after him" and then old Big-nose would choke on his mutton and say "squealing like a banshee." All through supper. Except he never did actually choke, all the way, I mean, more's the pity. Anyway it was a painful experience. I went out to see Charlie after supper. He's still extremely agitated. Oh, Diary, how can people be so insensitive?

I wish somebody would shoot Baldy Jonasson.

1925, Children playing in Lake Winnipeg.

Saturday, November 11, 1950

Dear Diary,

The good news is we're going to visit Auntie Imba and Uncle Jorindur in Ashern tomorrow. Auntie Imba has an electric refrigerator and she buys recipe books in Winnipeg. No canned mutton in her kitchen, you bet! I told Big-nose Alex that while we go to Ashern he can eat all the hay he wants. He told me to stop clucking.

The bad news is that Mom found another Icelandic book and she says I have to read 20 pages of it a day. It's called *Kristin Lavransdöttir*. This is supposed to be some kind of Icelandic classic, whatever that means. At least so far there haven't been any yellow chickens.

Sunday, November 12, 1950

Dear Diary,

Well, we went to Ashern. Coffee cakes, cookies, fudge and cinnamon buns. David ate too much as usual. Food is all that horrid boy can think about. Einar says I read stupid books. I told Einar that my book may be Icelandic but it's still better than the Eaton's catalogue.

But I have just done a very terrible thing. I read a little bit more than 20 pages, just by accident, in *Kristin Lavransdöttir*. And now Mom refuses to listen when I try to explain to her how much I really don't like it.

David and Einar are playing Dad's Bing Crosby records. They are also singing along. It's a good thing Charlie can't hear them or he'd really think he was being murdered. I'm going downstairs to sit with Amma. Those poems of hers sound better than my kid brothers at least.

P.S. We each got a chocolate bar from Uncle Jurindur's hardware story yesterday. I'm saving mine for the next time we have mutton.

Gimli, Remembered

David Arnason

I grew up in Gimli on the fulcrum of a shift from the old to the new, from the age of the pioneers to the contemporary age. My father was a fisherman on Lake Winnipeg, and my earliest memories are of the smell of nets soaked in bluestone and hanging in the basement in the fall, newly varnished corks strung on lines and the gasoline scent of outboard motors. During the depression of the thirties, my father had worked filleting fish for Armstrong Fisheries. He lifted his own nets before dawn and worked until dark filletting fish. I was amazed at his skill with a knife. He hauled fish out of boxes and filleted them so fast his hands were a blur. The nets were cotton then, and they couldn't simply be left in the lake. They had to be taken out and spread on the lawn to dry before they were set again. And in the time between seasons, there was "seaming-on," the gossamer seine tied to a sideline by big wooden needles, and the corks and leads attached.

The dock at Gimli then was a place of real excitement. Huge boats with names like the Goldfield and the Keenora arrived regularly to disgorge boxes of fish from the mysterious north of the lake, and they parked beside fishermen's boats (known as gasboats to distinguish them from the sail boats that had already disappeared from the lake). When the boats came in from the north, they invariably brought Indians and men who after months of isolation and hard work were anxious to celebrate.

In the winter, horses pulled cabooses made from light frames and tarpaper out onto the lake. These cabooses were often warmed by stoves, and odd chimneys protruded from them. Inside, the men stored the chisels and jiggers that they needed to set their nets under the ice. The odd fisherman even stuck with dog teams and sleds. Later,

as new technologies edged their way in, there were converted war-surplus Bren gun carriers on the lake. I remember, too, an odd invention called an ice plane. It was a small aerodynamic shed on skis that was pushed by an airplane propeller. Even now, it would look futuristic. I don't suppose they were all yellow, but as I try to remember them, I can think of no other colour.

We fished and farmed, like a lot of other families. I grew up in a world of horses, where the tractor was reserved for heavy work, like plowing. We mowed and raked hay with horses, and we used a sweep and a stacker to make haystacks. We loaded the hay onto hayracks with pitchforks, and raised it with slings into the hayloft of the barn, which was red and white, as all self-respecting barns were in those days. We milked cows twice a day, and in winter, we shovelled the manure from the barn onto a sleigh and hauled it to the manure pile.

Rural electrification hit the area around Gimli in 1948. Before that, we lit our houses with coal-oil lamps, heated them with wood or coal furnaces, and cooked over wood stoves. We didn't get waterworks until the mid-fifties, and we were earlier than most of our neighbours. Until then, we used outdoor toilets furnished with old Eaton's and Simpson's catalogues, and I learned a severe and ascetic discipline. People of my generation do not dawdle in the toilet. The threat of frostbite lingers long after central heating.

In the forties and well into the fifties, there was no doubt of Gimli's ethnic shape. In the stores and on the streets you heard more Icelandic and Ukrainian than English. In the Lakeside Trading Company on the corner of Centre and Main, you could buy anything from nails and

Fred Arnason with cows at Espihóll.
Photo from the collection of Herman Arnason in
the archives of Terry Tergesen.

harness to dried apples and cleaning supplies. It was a general store that took the word "general" seriously. Here business was generally conducted in Icelandic. If you walked down to Kasupski's a block away, commerce was almost exclusively handled in Ukrainian.

My parents were not anxious that I or any of my brothers and sisters speak Icelandic. I suppose they didn't want us to sound like immigrants. In the forties, the displaced people from Europe were highly visible, and in spite of their misfortune, largely seen as a threat to Canadian jobs and Canadian society. You didn't want to sound like a "D.P." I learned anyway, from my grandparents, but it was a kind of furtive exercise that made me proficient in farm language and in the expressions you need to speak to animals, but largely hopeless in other realms. I am still most comfortable speaking Icelandic with four-year-olds on farms.

Our schoolbooks were largely the books of Empire, conjuring a world ruled by the benevolent British and inhabited by a bewildering succession of Kings and Queens. Those textbooks were unabashedly racist, jingoistically patriotic to the British crown, and out of date by about fifty years. We were being trained to live in a world that no longer existed. And it was a bewildering world. The Britain of our textbooks might as well have been Mars. And of course there were no British in Gimli except for the Bristows, and they seemed as Icelandic as anyone else, having inter-married and having no support anywhere in the community for British ways.

My earliest memories are tied to the Second World War and to uncles in scratchy air-force uniforms with funny hats. I had my own ration book, which made me a person of some importance, and I remember my deep dismay as my lovely coupons disappeared. To make up for the loss, I was dressed in small military uniforms. I was the envy of all the boys in my class at school when I appeared in breeches with a head-fitting aviator's cap complete with goggles. The goggles were of a plastic that immediately went cloudy and cracked in thirty-below weather, but I wore them anyway.

Talk was always of the war, and though I discovered later that the Icelandic community was divided about the virtues of the war, the numbers of relatives I had in uniform made it certain that our family was in it to win. In fact, during both wars, the Icelanders in Canada were a lot more decided in their loyalties than those in the old country. Iceland itself had historic ties to Germany, and the First

World War had brought Iceland unheard-of prosperity supplying fish and mutton and sheepskins for the forces allied against the Germans. The Canadian Icelanders generally felt that they owed their new country their loyalty, and they had enlisted out of proportion to their numbers. Laura Goodman Salverson's *The Viking Heart* conjures up the power and the tragedy of that commitment.

Those who opposed the First World War argued that it was Britain's problem and that Icelanders were fools to die in it. The Second World War seemed less an European war to which Canadians were being needlessly drawn, and the Icelandic-Canadians had begun to think of themselves as less Icelandic and more Canadian. Besides, Hitler and Naziism seemed a clear moral danger, an unthinkable cancer on civilization that needed to be uprooted. To fight Hitler was not fight anybody else's battle. A nameable and definable evil was abroad, and we were all in the fray together.

The Icelandic community in Gimli, whatever it might have thought on the subject of war, was a peaceful group. There was very little local crime, and in fact, the original constitution of New Iceland made no provision for criminal law, presumably on the assumption that there would be no law-breaking. Icelandic-Canadian children were raised permissively, seldom spanked or even spoken to harshly. Few doors in Gimli, and fewer still in Arborg or Riverton, were ever locked until the fifties. Few even had locks. And not a few remain unlocked, even today. My grandmother, who was born here in 1896, remembers that travellers would often show up at the door late at night, looking for a meal and somewhere to stay. They were never turned away, even if the woman of the house were home alone, and she remembers no evil coming of this practice.

And we did grow up knowing about New Iceland. Icelanders are deeply interested in their genealogy, and of course in the history of their ancestors. The history of the founding of New Iceland was almost an obsession of my

1945, Centre Street, east of First Avenue, Gimli, Manitoba.

grandparents, and now apparently of me as well. For years, Ingi Bjarnason was the janitor of the Gimli school. And after classes, for years, he taught Icelandic language and the history of New Iceland to a handful of children whose parents felt they should know these things.

That school was also inhabited by Miss Stefánsson, who graduated from the University of Manitoba in 1915 and literally took possession of the school and town as the main source of education, intellectualism and moral force for the next fifty years. She taught us English and French (I can still bewilder Parisians with my accent) and there is hardly a student who graduated from Gimli before 1965 who doesn't remember a special relationship with her. She was the kind of powerful, intellectual woman who has characterized both Icelandic and Icelandic-Canadian communities. When she was frail and elderly, she took a bus to Washington D.C. to march in a civil-rights demonstration, a show of moral commitment that still matters to us all. It was rumoured that she had never married because of the tragic death of a lover in the First World War and her desire to remain true to his memory. There is no way of knowing now, but I choose to believe that version. It's what she would have done.

My mother, too, told stories of a powerful woman teacher who had influenced her. The woman was Salóme Halldórson, who taught at the Jón Bjarnason Academy, an Icelandic private school in Winnipeg. My mother was a brilliant young woman who skipped two grades in elementary school, and found herself at the age of eleven having completed the eight grades available to her there. At just that time, her father died unexpectedly. She sat out of school for a year, but her brothers, at considerable personal sacrifice, sent her to Winnipeg to study the following year. There she encountered Salóme Halldórson an early feminist and rigorous intellectual, and a demanding but exciting teacher. Miss Halldórson went on to become a Social Credit member of the Manitoba Legislature and an early supporter of the Voice of Women.

The Icelandic community has always been proud of the contributions of women. In the 1890s, a group of women from Gimli published *Svava,* an early feminist magazine, and Icelandic women were prominent in the women's suffrage movement in Manitoba. One of Gimli's most popular mayors, Viólet Einarson, ruled in a period when there were few women in municipal politics. The Icelandic sagas are filled with images of powerful and self-assured women, and the Canadian-Icelanders love to talk about that heritage. Nevertheless, the pioneering experience forced both men and women into traditional roles, and the women in Gimli felt quite as oppressed as their sisters in other communities in Canada.

But always, education and culture were the central values in the Canadian-Icelandic community. I remember knowing that it was a thing to be proud of that Gimli had two newspapers within a couple of years of its founding. All the Icelandic families I knew had bookcases filled with books, and reading was not merely entertainment. It was what made you civilized. The town was fiercely proud of the Kristjánson's because five brothers from a single family had received Ph.D.'s. I remember when I was in grade one, Mr. Menzies, the school inspector came to talk to our class, fifty-one tiny scholars under the tutelage of Miss Thórðarson. He told us that only three of us would make it to university. By that time, I had been so indoctrinated with the aim of education, that I, in my youthful arrogance, wondered only who the other two would be, and what those who stayed home would do.

Writing was important. It was a good thing to be a poet in a time when poets were not much valued. Every *Íslendingadagurinn,* poets climbed onto the stage at the Gimli Park and read their work to the gathered faithful. Music was equally important, not so much music that was imported via recordings and radio, but music that was performed by local performers, and we had our own little pantheon of stars.

Everything came to a head with the Icelandic celebration,

the *Íslendingadagurinn,* unpronounceable to non-Icelanders, but a day that was more important than Christmas in our calendar. In retrospect, it's hard to remember precisely what we did then. We raced in the children's races and watched our parents in the comic spectacles of the three-legged race and the sack race. We ate hot dogs and drank coke while our parents ate hardfish. Mostly, we visited. We met distant and exotic cousins, and the children of family friends who had moved away a long time ago. We went to people's houses and ate vínarterta and rúllupylsa and skyr. We listened to the soft sing-song of Icelandic, and we were sure that, on that day at least, we were at the centre of the universe. There was only one place anyone could want to be, and that was Gimli.

1956, commercial fishing in Selkirk.

Tornado and Thingvalla Lutheran.
Photo by Wayne Gudmundson.

Two White Churches

Wayne Gudmundson

"When can we eat?" my brother and I ask as we pull out of the drive of our south Moorhead home.

"Not until we pass the airport," my Norwegian mother replies. With the airport still in the rearview mirror, the peanut butter and jelly sandwiches are reduced to crumbs and assorted small stains in the back seat of the family's red and white '54 Chevy.

"Now, how many miles to Mountain?" we demand.

"About 180."

"Oh," we sigh as we enter purgatory again.

Without turning around my mother repeats the chant: "We'll be in Mountain after we pass the two white churches."

Finally, there on the east side of the road stubbornly stand Thingvalla Lutheran, nondescript except for the fieldstone monument just to the north with the bas relief bronze bust of K.N. Jullus (1860-1936).

We know, but we ask again who the guy is on the stone marker. Smiling, no doubt because we are so close to Mountain, but also because of the memory, my Icelandic father says, "Ahh . . . that's old K.N. He was a gravedigger, a handyman, and a poet."

Down the gully, over the small, drooling stream, left past Borg old folks home, we finally take a sweeping right turn and look up the wide main street of Mountain. Even in the 50s each trip back brought news of another business gone, another family moved, another death. But, of course, to a six-year-old, this information was as interesting as the chemical makeup of the white paint on the pine boards of Vikur Lutheran, the end point of our journey.

In 1878 Reverend Páll Thorláksson, seeking a site for his religious followers to establish a new community, along with his group picked a rocky rise on the west edge of the Red River Valley. By the autumn of 1879 about fifty families, most from Gimli in New Iceland, had settled in this area. There, from their infertile but dry perch nestled at the base of the Pembina escarpment, the Icelanders, like Puffins, could stare east over some of the best farming land in North America. In 1882 Thorláksson died at the age of thirty-three. Today his gravestone towers above the others in the cemetery on the land he donated to his church – Vikur Lutheran, the oldest Icelandic Church in America.

Kitty corner from Byron's bar, across from the Mountain Cash store and just over the ravine from Vikur Lutheran, stood my grandparents' house. We were always greeted with food – brown bread and cheese sandwiches, vinarterta, ponnukokur. My brother and I had unlimited access to the kleinur. There was laughter, lively discussions – always movement. Following our lunch, my Grandfather Chris, who once ran a livery service and later became Mountain's first used car salesman, would sweep us into his car for unending rounds of visiting from one house to the next, but each pilgrimage always included a stop at the farm of Árni and Rósa Johnson.

After the usual introductory exchanges the men and women would separate like oil and vinegar – the children, depending on age, became free agents wandering back and forth between the two conversational camps.

Rósa presided, moving as if she were under water, floating between her stove, refrigerator, and table with coffee, bread, pastries, all the while talking about how we'd grown, who we'd seen, how she and Stína, my grandmother, were best friends. Time held its breath. Forty years later, Rósa in her late 90s, for the third time says, "Now who are you?" Her daughter adds, "This is Eddie's son."

I ask of K.N. "Oh yes," Rósa returns. "Old K.N., with the stem of his pipe he would comb his grand mustache. He had a poem for everything. He stopped here for coffee every time he walked back from town. You know old K.N. lived at the Gier place just a mile south of here. He had the upstairs bedroom. From there he could see the church where he dug graves. Ah . . . now who are you?"

It was in Árni's vinegary corner, that I was first introduced

Vikur Lutheran.
Photo by Wayne Gudmundson.

to poetry. The men would take turns reciting K.N.'s poems in Icelandic, at which point they might nod and, while inhaling, say softly "Yow, yow." Or, torn with laughter they would bellow, "Yow, that's a good one, but have you heard about the time K.N. was walking home and a Model-T went by and splashed mud on him? He instantly made a poem against this fellow. It went like this . . ."

Occasionally certain poems were spoken in English for us young ones in the crowd who were brought up to be "Americans" and knew no Icelandic.

The first poem I remember hearing was said by my father to the group:

Brennan
Nú legg eg hönd, á helga bók
og henni í eldinn fleygi.
Drottinn gaf og drottinn tók; –
en djöfullinn segir "holy smoke"
– eg hljóður hugsa og þegi.

Burning
Now I lay my hands on the holy book
And I throw it in the fire.
The Lord gave and the Lord took
And the Devil says Holy Smoke,
I quietly think and remain silent.

I remember thinking as a six-year-old that being a man night be ok – sitting with friends speaking a mysterious language, reciting and enjoying poetry which poked fun at people, politicians, and the church.

But of course, even then I knew the good poems stayed in K.N.'s native tongue.

K.N.'s first book, *Kviðlingar,* was printed in Winnipeg in 1920. *Kviðlingar Og Kvæði,* edited by Richard Beck, appeared in Reykjavik in 1945, and *Vísnabók Káins,* edited by Tómas Guðmundsson, was published in 1988 – all in Icelandic. He is revered and his work memorized in Iceland but for most of his life in Mountain he was tolerated as a familiar scallywag.

K.N.'s work defined a secular community conscience and at the same time he recorded the vitality of that pioneer town in its heyday.

Árni Johnson said that in the 1920s you could get anything you wanted in Mountain – a railroad served the community, a fire hall, a pool hall, hotel, general stores, livery stables, a bank and bars – there was no need to leave. Today the biggest business is Borg old folks home, followed by Byron's Bar.

My Mountain then, and to a large extent the ghost of Mountain today, exists between the spirits of the men buried at the two white churches.

Each of our visits would include a trip to the hill west of town. At the top, Grandpa Chris would turn the Chevy (later Fords) around and stop. Adult talk would float over the constant breeze . . . "the Cafe is closing . . . August the Deuce was pretty crazy again . . . the new paster Olafur Skúlason from Reykjavík will do ok." Then Grandpa Chris would make the signal that we in the back seat had been suffering silently for: "Well, how far do you think we can go?" Guesses were made. Brake off, clutch in, we were off. The car gained speed, bouncing us along the steep, rough road, our adrenaline pumping. Then, all too soon we reached the bottom and the inevitable slowing – past the telephone pole, in and out of the gully, the mailbox inching toward us, and finally the quiet stop.

Today the mountain has been cut into, the ascending road widened and the smoother coasting road paved. Still, following the adult talk and the click of a shutter, I ask my wife, Jane, seated beside me holding our two-month-old daughter, Liv, "Well, how far do you think we can go?" Brake off, clutch in, we coast past familiar landmarks, the signs and symbols of other days, into Mountain, past the old A.O.U.W. Hall, down the incline, through the stop sign and out onto that endless open space, finally coming to rest a mile below town. Chris would have liked it – a new record.

The end of Main Street, Mountain, North Dakota.
Photo by Wayne Gudmundson.

The Icelanders in Minneota

Bill Holm

Icelanders do not leave monuments, in the old world or in the new. Both here and there, their numbers are small – and their genius never included the amassing of property, or the making of great cathedrals or mansions, or the erection of triumphal arches to commemorate their victories over nature or anything else. Against nature, they always lost: ice, volcanic ash, and isolation in the old world; mosquitoes, winter, bank failures in the new. They built from sod and cheap wood and their buildings hardly outlasted them. Their only real monuments are in language, story, reputation, myth and a few names – the invisible world, but as we are always reminded by our religion, our philosophy, our moralists, the only lasting world, and the only real substance.

I was born in Minneota – which old Icelanders in my childhood identified as an Icelandic town. After all, Icelanders lived there. That alone made it an Icelandic place. The two thirds or three fourths of the town that were Norwegian, Belgian, German, Irish, and whatever else, hardly raised their voices in protest. But what good would it have done them if they had? The Icelanders were not listening . . .

This is only a small exaggeration. All humans imagine themselves the centre of the universe wherever or whoever they are. We are spiritual Solipsists to a fault. It underlies our wars and our ravings and rantings at each other over matters that are none of each other's business. Connected to military or economic power, that habit of mind becomes bloody and destructive, but for Icleanders, unconnected to any power but language, whether in talk or on the page, it was only comic and sweetly eccentric.

I moved back to Minneota, my birthplace, at about forty, because it seemed to me as good a place for metaphor as any on earth. What more useful human metaphor than an Icelandic emigrant? For a while after I returned, the local monuments of my boyhood were still mostly intact, and I took visitors on a whimsical "grand tour": a fine old round barn, a dry goods store pickled in the 1890s and still intact, some literate, elderly, first-speakers-of-Icelandic with well stocked bookshelves, a lonesome and lovely old country church on top of a windy hill. After fifteen years, age, death, and economic inconsequences have harvested them all and have made my grand tour completely a work of the imagination. It can be performed for the blind or on the radio or on paper as well as for you. It has disappeared from the world of stones and newspapers and canned goods into the solid ether of myth.

The last to go, on March 11 of this year, 1994, was the Lincoln County Icelandic Church. It closed twenty-five years ago. The Icelanders, stubborn but never devout, either neglected to marry and reproduce or else sent their children off to cities where there was a better market for language and fewer stones and thistles. A few windows cracked in hailstorms and wore plywood eye patches; blizzard winds lashed the white paint off most of the siding boards; its weathered porch rotted a foot away from the front door; arrogant weeds stuck out their necks between the foundation stones. The local Icelanders who owned land in the graveyard just north of the church faced two choices: either spend money to restore the church as a useless monument – but a lovely one – or tear it down before it fell in on itself or burned. Lincoln County offered them a third choice and they took it. They sold the church for one dollar to the county museum in Hendricks, 14 miles west on the South Dakota border. On a cold sunny March morning the church deserted its foundation forever and rode in slow and stately procession down county roads to its new home – now neighbour to an old depot, a country school, and a farmhouse. No longer Icelandic, it had done what its parishioners did in the last generation: become a genuine American – whatever that means and whatever its consequences. It left, as the poet Tom Hennen says, "a hole in the landscape," a real hole, but that nevertheless one can "walk through it and back again." The invisible doesn't cease to exist, as both the ancient Icelandic poets and the American transcendentalists well knew.

The Lincoln County church was one of three founded in the 19th century to service the cultural and religious needs of the Icelandic emigrants who began arriving in western Minnesota in 1875. A farmer named Gunnlaugur Petturson was the first. He made his way to a farm northeast of Minneota after giving Wisconsin a try – our original "land taker." More Icelanders began filtering into the Minneota area immediately afterwards. The heavy years of settlement were 1878–1882, and by the turn of the century the immigration had for all real purposes stopped. A few stragglers filtered here in the 20th century, but Minneota and the surrounding townships basically reached their present form in 1900. The slide has been downhill toward the rest of America since then – as an Icelander might put it.

What moved Icelanders out of the maritime Arctic to the continental sub-Artic? Why would a human being give up language, culture, mountains, sheep, history after stubbornly lasting through a thousand years? Food, land, and an easier future, presumably, though all the land takers are now dead and can't be asked. The prime cause for most Minneota Icelanders was the catastrophic eruption of the volcano Askja in 1875. Lava flows buried most of Jökuldal, and ash covered and poisoned the pastures, killing the sheep all over northeast Iceland. The majority of Minneota immigrants came from the tiny isolated weapon fjörð: Vopnafjörður, and the farms just south of it in Hérað by

The Big Store, the immigrant Icelanders's great commercial success dressed up with flags for July 4. Taken before 1915 when the "new" wing was added. Photo courtesy S.W. Minnesota History Center.

Interior of the Big Store, the Icelandic Eaton's of Minneota, about 1920. It was state of the art for 1900 and stayed pickled that way until 1975. Photo courtesy S.W. Minnesota History Center.

Lagarfljót. The boats filled up fast leaving Seyðisfjörður for Liverpool, then Quebec, then the long train to Winnipeg, then the wagon or the two feet.

When they bought or homesteaded land around Minneota, they were frequently swindled by the railroad acting as land agent. They founded churches – in rural Westerheim Township, in Lincoln County west of Minneota, and a grander mother church in Minneota itself. They hired Icelandic ministers and quarreled about theology. Some

Icelanders in Canada and North Dakota left the Lutherans to become rational Unitarians, but Minneota stayed Lutheran by becoming Unitarian in spirit of tolerance. It was home to free-thinkers, the disagreeable, and the heterodox. That is the way churches are supposed to be – houses for the spirit, not for right opinions (whatever *they* might be). They founded a cooperative store including (of course!) the first bookstore in the area, but mostly, they gradually made their way off farms and into the world, not of

The Big Store float, 1914. A roadster bedecked with tissue, roses, and a gala pennet. Photo courtesy S.W. Minnesota History Center.

The annual Big Store float, this time with a naval motif, just before the Unites States's entry into W.W.I. Photo courtesy S.W. Minnesota History Center.

business, but of language. They founded the town newspaper, *The Minneota Mascot,* wrote it, printed it, and made it one of the distinguished and influential small town weeklies in Minnesota. They became lawyers and judges in numbers far out of proportion to the size of the community. They pooled their money and sent their cleverest children off to universities where they became teachers and journalists. They used their skill in oratory and public speech to become politicians – mayors, state legislators, and officials. They exhibited the restlessness of their history in Europe by traveling – moving all over America and Canada to pursue adventure, success, sometimes just to keep moving, coming home only to one of the three Icelandic graveyards.

They learned English quickly and anglicized their names to avoid embarrassing their neighbours: Kjartan Eðvarðson became Charlie Edwards, Bjarni Jónsson became became Barney Jones, Jóhannes Halldórsson became Jack Frost, Griðjón Gunnlaugur Jóhannesson became John Holme. They gave their children classical and literary patronymics names: Io, Olympia, Voltaire, to replace the old Viking ones. They gave up their old country patronymics and took citizenship names like Stone, Jokull, Holm, Benson, Johnson, Eastman, Gilbertson, Strand. Almost Episcopalian, true WASP names.

Centuries after they had given up their reputation as pillagers of the European continent, they learned to fight again for their new county. They went off to defend American against Spanish aggression within twenty years of getting here, and twenty years later went off again to dig Europe out of the trenches in Belgium and France. After "seeing Paree" they left the farm in great numbers, married outside the tribe, and came home only to visit and bury the old. I think Icelanders never liked crop farming. They were animal tenders whom the regular boredom of weeding and seeding drove with even greater intensity to make their way in the world with language. Most of the Icelandic farms are Belgian now, owned by grandsons of farmers who took soil more seriously than as a source for sheep fodder and poetry.

They made a little civilization – while it lasted – and I was born in 1943 into the tail end of it. The old people who had stayed in Minneota were demonstrably *not* American, either in habit of mind or in accent, and I loved them for their stubborn strangeness. The Icelanders still owned the "Big Store," Minneota's Eaton's or Dayton's. They ran the *Mascot* and they mayored the town. The public speeches for Memorial Day, 4th of July, and school graduations were delivered by eminent Icelanders – Valdimar Björnson, a successful journalist and politician, or Sidney Gíslason, an eminent attorney. While other immigrants chased money or bought land, the Icelanders mostly did the talking – and the writing – for the town and I suppose that had something to do with my own life as a "language" man.

An astonishing number of Icelanders never married – sometimes creating whole large families of bachelors and spinsters. Why, I've asked for years? The answers shift as in a kaleidoscope – shyness, parental compulsion to marry Icelanders rather than Catholics, duty to aged parents, inertia, fear, stubborness. There's no certain answer. But as a result, this little culture flourished awhile then evaporated into history and memory. Not a bad place to go, but a quiet one.

What's left in Minneota of the once flourishing, noisy, and successful Icelandic immigrant culture? The Icelandic church, its congregation now old – very old – clings stubbornly to life. The new parishioners are not Icelanders, and not – justly – much interested in them. The Big Store still stands, its sales floor a used furniture storeroom and the old Opera house upstairs a half-finished town museum that's run out of steam for the moment. A few farms are still farmed by oldest sons who felt some duty and pleasure in their grandfather's land. A few names still decorate the phone book though in shriveled numbers: Gíslason, Josephson, Magnúson, Ousman, Askdal, Rafnson, Hofteig,

Guttormsson, Guðmundson. There are a lot of half, quarter, and eighth Icelanders left – even Catholic ones – who still call themselves Icelanders – with, I think, some ironic pride. It's an odd thing to *be* in America and so they claim it. It's curious that as in the 19th and early 20th century a tiny drop of Negro blood would make you legally and socially Black, so the same tiny drop makes you an Icelander. I have a few acquaintances with both Black and Icelandic blood. It must be a terrible conflict for them! But a real American one, nevertheless. Here you are what you call yourself – whether it's the right name or not.

And little Bill Holm is left – come home to a home that has almost disappeared around him, home to make inconsequential metaphors in honour of a mostly inconsequential blip in the history of humans wriggling around on this planet. They will not quite *get* these metaphors in California, or in Toronto, but I make them anyway – to pass the time. I sometimes think it's a genetic curse and a blessing together – some ghost Icelander from the east fjords brushing my ear with his supernatural, snuff-encrusted mustache whispering "Say something – anything; just keep faithful to language and nothing can ever entirely disappear."

Though Icelanders in Minneota are now on their way to pure history, that history sometimes haunts them in odd ways. Christian Günter Schram, himself a German emigrant to Iceland, left a dead first wife and first family in the old country, emigrated to Minneota in the 1880s already in his 50s, married again, started a new batch of children, worked as a carpenter and merchant, prospered, and died at a ripe old age in 1914, just as the mind of Europe was beginning to bury itself in its long dank trenches. When I was a boy, the only ghost of the Schrams was an old lady, Sara Kline, poor and eccentric. One of Schram's nephews had fathered a child with her, and his grave was off at an angle from the big white Schram stone in the Icelandic graveyard just south of Minneota. Sara led a damaged and lonesome life as a kind of bag lady, scrounging cigarette butts and serviceable garbage. My mother ordered me kiss her and greet her in Icelandic and when she died in the 50s, I sang at her funeral. That was my only acquaintance with what I thought the finished name: Schram. But when I went to Iceland in 1978, I met a beautiful woman named Bryndís Schram. She was a former Icelandic beauty queen, presently an actress, and the wife of a famous Icelandic politician. Making small talk at a party, I told her I recognized her name from an American tombstone. "You must be from Minneota," she said. "That was my great grandfather. I came from the first wife who died in Iceland."

I said something sharp and witty like "Small world!" and thought to myself that, as usual, it was the just work of a cliché to be true.

Now, in 1994, sixteen years after that meeting, a young fellow named Kristján Gunnar Schram arrived at the parsonage in Minneota to arrange his marriage to an American woman, Elizabeth Nunberg, from Minneapolis. Kristján was his great, great grandfather's namesake (in its true Icelandic spelling), and wanted to be married in the only place in North America connected to him by blood and history. And so, on a fine windy June afternoon, the old Icelandic church that the original Christian helped build, worshipped in and was buried from, held more Schrams. It became a kind of swinging bridge between the old world and the new, between past and present, between history and metaphor.

We may never, in fact, be done with being Icelanders here in Minneota. It may be as with Walt Whitman's *Leaves of Grass,* never finished, only waiting for the appearance of new songs from another world when we've finally figured out how to understand them.

I'll close this little essay – or sermon – with two poems, one about the Icelanders in America, and one about an American in Iceland. They say what this essay tries to say, in another form. Maybe that's what it means to be an Icelander, to keep saying what you see till it comes right and moves on to others.

The Icelandic Emigration to Minneota, Minnesota

Bill Holm

I

After only a thousand years where they were,
In Vopnafjörður, Flói and Jökuldal,
They left again, some for coffee, some for land,
Some no doubt for the hell of it, and came here.
They did not keep slaves, did not get capital,
Did not open any more wilderness. They farmed,
Grumbled, voted Republican, said their Rs wrong,
Dreamed in genders. A few went out to the barn
With ropes, but from another few it dropped away
So quickly that after a few years you could
Not tell them from the others. By the next
Generation the names went wrong in the neighbours'
Mouths; the R slipped off the teeth, and slid back
Into the throat. The dreams came in genders now
Only after whiskey, or when the last disease
Fastened its baling hook deep into the brain.

II

In the third generation, all that was left:
Sweet cake, small stories, a few words whose meaning
Slunk away to die under the mental stone
That buries all the lost languages in America.
The Mayans are there, Pequod and Penobscot,
And the Mandingo, and the Delaware Swedes.
The first tongue lost, did they acquire another?
The language of marketing and deterring
For the language of fish, poverty and poems?
In *The Invasion of the Body Snatchers,*
Seed pods open in your own closet at night,
Metastasizing into a body in-
distinguishable from your own, but the brain
Is something new, without memory, without
Passion, without you. Is this what it's like
To become a whole American at last?

c. 1900, Minneota, Minnesota. Two Americanized Icelanders, Barney Jones (formerly Bjarni Jónsson) and his wife, Stefanía Jones, after 15 years in the New World. Photos courtesy Bill Holm.

Vietnamese Cooking in Reykjavík

Bill Holm *(for Teng Gee and Jón)*

(When the boat people arrived at the airport in Iceland, the Icelandic Red Cross gave them one red rose and a new Icelandic name to memorize. The Immigrants carried those cards with them at all times to remind them.)

He is half my size, tight olive face,
a quick body, called Gunnar
in this new place, a name
he neither can remember
nor pronounce. He sways
in front of garlic, rubbing off
dry skin, whacking the bud
with a flat knife. "For juice,"
he says brokenly, and smiles.
He knows what his name is
though he carries
GUNNAR, in block letter
in the pocket of his Red
Cross corduroy pants.

Wok oil smokes. His two knives
work the garlic, mincing it
into snow. It bounces
in boiling oil. He nods.
Next come tiny haystacks
of onion, cabbage, pork, shrimp;
he trims a woody broccoli stalk,
the last of an Icelandic garden.
"This is no good," he points,
"but *this* good." Pale green
broccoli soon is paper-thin
under his knives. To women
you love you could write:
"you are beautiful," in delicate

calligraphy on these pale
leaves of broccoli paper. He looks
into the pan, knows he had invented
something beyond language.

We mumble to each other thanks
and praise in Icelandic pidgin.
What a strange earth! To slide us:
immigrant and emigrant into this
arctic kitchen, then give us only
food for words; one language gone,
the other not yet born, the third:
mingling boiled fish smells
with sesame, coriander, garlic.
Outside, a mean-tempered wind
slices over the Denmark Strait
blows the sea under the door jamb,
cold, salt, and bitter; water
that carries us wherever
we drift on earth, and back again.

Have You Seen the Jólasveinar?

Leigh Syms

Illustrations by Stefan Tergesen

The Icelandic heritage is rich in traditions of strange beings such as the following account of the thirteen Jólasveinar (Christmas giants, or sometimes described as little people). The following is for children and the young at heart with imaginative minds. The Jólasveinar were described in various households in North American communities, such as Langruth, in the early years of this century. The retelling of their activities renews an old Icelandic heritage and adds another dimension to Christmas in addition to the spiritual element and the excitment of Santa Claus.

A great variety of unusual creatures with magical powers has been seen around the world. This was particularly true long ago, but there are still places where some people see "little folk," fairies, mischievous imps, dwarfs, witches and giants. Only people who believe in them will see them. It has been said that every time a child says, "I don't believe in fairies!," one of those wee, delicate creatures grows sad and sickly and fades away into a puff of dust.

Iceland has been the home of many strange and magical creatures – little people, giants and ogresses! One group is the Jólasveinar – the thirteen mischievous giants who appear just before Christmas. Have you seen them? When they appear in the countryside of Iceland, they pull many naughty pranks.

If you are awake, very late on December 12th, you may see "Stiff-Legged Sheep Chaser," the first giant to appear. He loves to chase the sheep and other farm animals in order to make them upset and confused. Because of him the farm animals must be rounded up again.

"Gorge Oaf" appears on the night of December 13th. He sneaks into the milking barns with a sly look and steals the creamy froth from the fresh warm milk. Some of the bubbly magic of the milk is lost, forever.

On the evening of the 14th, rolly-polly "Shorty" visits the kitchens. He delights in borrowing full kitchen pans and cleaning them in order to fill his ever-empty tummy.

"Spoon Licker" appears on the 15th. He is tall and lean – a skinny stick of a giant! Food left in the kitchen is his goal.

Fifth is "Pot Scraper" who tries to eat all of the leftovers before the children can. Pieces of cake, bits of pudding, skyr and other delicacies to which the children have been looking forward disappear.

"Pot Licker" arrives on December 17th. He hides under the bed and creeps out to steal food. He even stoops so low as to steal food from the pets.

On the 18th you are likely to hear "Door Slammer." He enjoys disturbing everyone's sleep.

The eighth giant arrives to stuff himself with dairy products. Milk, cheese, butter and skyr are in grave danger of disappearing.

"Sausage Stealer" arrives on the 20th. He tries to finish off all the smoked sausage that has been prepared for Christmas. Smoked sausages, bacon, rúllupylsa and hangikjöt may disappear in a flash.

On the 21st, "The Peeper" who is the 10th giant comes to frighten children and to steal presents. Christmas gifts and toys may disappear if children try to hide under their beds.

"The Sniffer" is number eleven. He arrives on the 22nd and, with his sensitive nose, sniffs out food to fill his skinny body.

If you listen very carefully on the evening of the 23rd you may hear "Meat Hooker" walking along the roof. He reaches down the chimney with his hook to snag meat that has been left out overnight.

Finally, on the 24th of December, "Candle Beggar" arrives to steal children's candles. He cannot resist taking unattended candles that are left burning.

A greedy lot they are! Their mischievous pranks can do much to spoil Christmas. Food and presents must carefully be put away. If children are good and do as they are told, the Jólasveinar can do little harm.

The Jólasveinar are best known in the isolated mountainous area of Iceland. Many of their activities there may be hidden by fog. However, they do appear wherever groups of Icelanders live and believe in them. Do they also reside in the low-lying areas of Hecla Island or Riverton in the Manitoba Interlake? Are they to be seen near Langruth, Wynyard, Gimli, Arborg, Minneapolis, Brandon, Seattle Markerville or other communities?

They will be seen only if you believe in them. Beware, and be good and they will do no harm.

Icelandic Canadian Literature

Viðar Hreinsson

"Þessi bók er sannkallaður fjandans þvættingur hana á með réttu bóndinn Benedikt Jónsson á Síðu í Víðidal. Efni: Sagan af Sigurði fót og Ásmundi Húnakóngi, Hermannssaga og Jallmanns, Konráðssaga keisarasonar, Gjafa Refssaga, Hrólfssaga Gutrekssonar, Fertramssaga og Plató, Úlfssaga Uggasonar, Dinusarsaga drambláta."

(This book is truly a damned rubbish, its true owner is the farmer Benidikt Jónsson of Síða in Víðidalur. Contents: . . . various legendary sagas/romances.)

These words are from the title page of one of the numerous manuscripts the usually poor settlers brought with them to North America. Only a very few of these manuscripts are still extant, most of them in the Icelandic Collection of the Elizabeth Dafoe Library at the University of Manitoba. The preserved manuscripts are typical of the various literary activities of the Icelanders in the 18th and 19th centuries, the result of the unusually widespread literacy in Iceland in this period, higher than in any other country. Probably the mentioned book of entertaining romances, was accompanied with another manuscript with a few rímur and poetry, perhaps some by the self-educated but physically handicapped Guðmundur Bergþórsson, who was a "kraftaskáld" but the tragedy of his life was that he was never able to curse away his own deformity. A book of psalms, Bible and *Vídalínspostilla* were the religious part of the literary luggage. *Vídalínspostilla* is a book of sermons written in such a powerful figurative language that it kept the whole nation awake during the evening-wake reading for centuries and it was important in maintaining the language intact. Books of practical instructions in farming, an ABC, a book of Jónas Hallgrímsson's poetry, Sigurður Breiðfjörð's rímur, also found their way to the small libraries on a prominent place in the log cabins, drawing the attention of Lord Dufferin who spoke enthusiastically about this strange group of settlers owning hardly anything but books. Lord Dufferin said:

> In fact, I have not entered a single hut or cottage in the settlement which did not contain, no matter how bare the walls, or scanty its furniture, a library of twenty or thirty volumes; and I am informed that there is scarcely a child amongst you who cannot read and write. (Wilhelm Kristjanson, *The Icelandic People in Manitoba* Winnipeg: Wallingford 1965:74)

The manuscripts and the old printed books are worn and dirty, bearing the marks of many hard working hands. Humble looking books, but the words of the Icelandic philologist and poet Jón Helgason can also account for these books:

> An Icelandic man who wanders through the display rooms of the British Museum and there seeing illuminated books from many different countries, the snow white and the soiled vellum, adorned with the most beautiful pictures, might then perhaps think about the books of his country, poorly illuminated, dark, and frequently damaged. He then may recall that it may well be that the tattered Icelandic books may preserve information which may not necessarily be inferior to the information in the other books, and even that the damage may indicate that they have not laid around unused in some chest of drawers, to be only taken forth to delight the eyes of gentlemen, but rather that they have given encouragement and joy to many past generations. (Translated from *Handritaspjall*, Reykjavík: Menningarsjóður 1958: p. 27)

Ambitious and passionate for books and learning, the emigrants founded a school as soon as they settled, eager

This dish is no longer common in North America, though it is inexplicably still eaten in Iceland. Take as many lamb's heads as you need. Singe thoroughly to remove hair. Cut in half and remove extraneous material. Rinse thoroughly, then boil for 90 minutes in salted water. Remove eyes and teeth if your guests are squeamish, and serve, ½ head per person. This course should never be served as a surprise to guests.

to learn English. They founded the newspaper *Framfari* as well, in the middle of serious perils. The founding of the paper was prepared in the winter 1876-77, when the smallpox epidemic raged. The first issue was published September 10, 1877. *Framfari* suffered from financial difficulties and ceased publication in 1880. *Leifur* was founded in 1883 by the energetic Helgi Jónasson. *Leifur* was published from May 5, 1883 until June 4, 1886. *Leifur* and *Framfari* broke the ground for the newspapers, *Heimskringla* (founded 1886), and *Lögberg*, (founded 1888), as well as for various journals and magazines. A tradition of rivalry and disagreement soon developed, *Lögberg* was orthodox in religion and liberal in politics, *Heimskringla* was liberal in religious matters and conservative in politics. The rivalry resulted in furious and deadly poisonous debate, with varying force, until 1930. After that peace reigned and the papers merged in 1959. Today the weekly *Lögberg-Heimskringla* only fights itself.

The papers brought knowledge, news, practical information, political, religious and personal debate, literature and culture. Translations from English, which often were published separately, were even popular in Iceland. In fact the Icelandic Nobel Prize winner Halldór Laxness claimed them as his favourite childhood readings. Not all the poetry in the papers enjoyed such a good reputation in Iceland. The papers were, however, instrumental in the comparatively large amount of literature flowing out of Western-Icelandic pens. They were the main field for literature in the beginning, but soon books began to appear. The first book of poetry appeared in 1887, a tiny booklet of 14 pages published by Jóhann Magnús Bjarnason, containing three poems by himself, Sigurður Jón Jóhannesson and Kristinn Stefánsson. Jóhann Magnús was also the pioneer in publishing prose. In 1892 a collection of short stories and two poems appeared, *Sögur og kvæði*. The stories are charmingly naive and primitive, sincere attempts to describe various aspects of the emigration experience. He also wrote a number of plays.

In the period 1870-1900, well over a hundred authors published poetry and prose in the papers and books, according to a research conducted by Ms. Árný Hjaltadóttir. It is impossible to get to an exact number, as many who wrote under pseudonyms may have written under their own names as well. Poetry by Icelandic authors was also printed, as were a large number of translations. This is not a small achievement of a group of around 15000 emigrants.

Naturally, the literature covered a quality-scale from terrible to world-class. The bulk of the literature is a valuable cultural documentation, multifarious expressions of the experience of generations of emigrants and their descendants. We can read in papers and books numerous bad and mediocre memorial poems and festive poems, soft spoken romantic works, poetic descriptions of nature, symbolist plays, prose which was realist and critical, didactic and moralist, parodic and symbolical, and so on. Nationalistic romance, naive mythmaking, and an appraisal of the freedom and opportunities in the new world, were striking features in, for instance, the festive poems of Sigurbjörn Jóhannsson and Sigurður Jón Jóhannesson. Those two were typical, skilled verse-making farmers, able to compose poems for all possible festive occasions. It was compulsory to recite "Minni Íslands," "Minni Kanada" "Minni Vestur Íslendinga" on *Íslendingadagurinn* and other festive days. This was a kind of court poetry, portraying the "official" ideals, but the tragic, sinister aspects of the emigrant experience acquired a literary voice as well. In the new world, not everybody was able to enjoy the highly praised freedom and create his own destiny. Some struggled their whole life without ever gaining the riches of the promised land, some lost their moral values if they ever had any. Young men seduced innocent girls, some young girls were ashamed of their nationality, eager to hide it and an easy prey for the seductive Englishmen. This was the whirlwind of an abrupt cultural change, from the backwardness of remote Icelandic valleys to the booming city of Winnipeg. Jóhann Magnús Bjarnason expressed warm sympathy for those who lost those battles and he also portrayed silent, strong, viking-like heroes who survived. Poems like "Grímur frá Grund" and "Íslenskur sögunarmaður í Vesturheimi" are his classic portrayals of those who lost everything except their dignity. Gunnsteinn Eyjólfsson revealed his satirical wit, showing moral dissolution and urban decay in the short novel *Elenóra,* and unscrupulous politicians in the beginning and end of an unfinished novel. A series of down and out failures inhabit his humorous satirical stories about the anti hero Jón á Strympu in the short story trilogy "Hvernig ég yfirbugaði sveitarráðið," "Járnbrautanefndin" and "Tíund." Jón Runólfsson was a tender romanticising melancholic. Kristinn Stefánsson was an excellent and productive poet, mastering both romantic sorrow and sharp satire. Undína was the pen name for Helga Steinvör Baldvinsdóttir, a skillfull young woman who wrote love poetry full of pain and sorrow. Jakobína Johnson, daughter of Sigurbjörn Stefánsson, composed soft and tender descriptions of nature and human surroundings, often using themes of clipped wings, unfulfilled desires. The peak is however the magnificent and dangerously critical poetry of Stephan G. Stephansson, to which the hypocrites could only say that he was obscure and clumsy. The intellectual range of his poetry is simply amazing, although it was composed at work, and written down during the night. He gave voice and philosophical depth to the new experience of the emigrants, painted the landscape of Alberta in unequalled images, and he never hesitated to criticise his fellow countrymen and tell the priests off. At first he was not too well received by everyone in the east and west, but in his last years, he corresponded with the most progressive and promising intellectuals in Iceland as well as intelligent literary farmers like himself.

Some of his poems were indeed somewhat stiff in their majesty, but the opposite of such stiffness can be found in the fluent verses of K.N., Káinn, Kristján Níels Júlíus Jónsson. He was a farm hand all his life, an ever-drunk gravedigger. But he mastered the verse making traditions to such an extent that he could put everything into verse, sometimes humorous paradoxes and word-plays, sometimes mocking Western Icelandic slang and inserting English words and sentences. He wrote numerous reflections over booze and grave digging, farm chores, politics, religion, as well as tender, classical jewels for and about children, like this one:

> Síðan fyrst ég sá þig hér,
> sólskin þarf ég minna;
> gegnum lífið lýsir mér
> ljósið augna þinna.

> Since I first saw you here
> I need less sunshine
> The light of your eyes
> brightens my life.

But he did not have the ambitions of a "real" serious poet. Some of his quatrains are obviously composed on the spot, humorous answers to one or another inquiry or remark. To the woman scolding him for his drinking, which she claimed had prevented him from having a good wife, he replied:

> Gamli Bakkus gaf mér smakka
> gæðin bestu, öl og vín.
> Honum á ég það að þakka,
> að þú ert ekki konan mín.

In my prose translation:

> Old Bacchus gave me the taste of
> the best goods, beer and wine.
> I can be grateful to him
> that you are not my wife.

No wonder that, as Káinn himself says in one of his poems, joy and laughter reigned in hell when Satan started reading aloud from *Kviðlingar* (Káinn's first book of poetry).

Hardly any of the poets and writers mentioned above, had any formal schooling. Their intellectual background was the Icelandic literary tradition. The intellectuals, on the other hand, were mainly the editors, Gestur Pálsson, who

MYSOSTUR

Bring two gallons of milk just to boiling point, then let cool until lukewarm. Add 1 teaspoon of liquid rennet. Allow to set, then strain off curd. Reduce whey to 1 pint (about 8 hours boiling). Add 1 cup sugar, ½ cup heavy cream, and 3 tablespoons of butter. Cook slowly for about one half hour. Beat until smooth and creamy. It should look like thin peanut butter, and is eaten as a spread on bread.

died a year after he came to Winnipeg and Jón Ólafsson and Einar Hjörleifsson Kvaran, who both returned to Iceland. Later, the medical doctor, goodtemplar, editor, socialist, philantrophist, pacifist Sigurður Júlíus Jóhannesson arrived. There were many more, intellectuals and unschooled authors: Jónas A Daníelsson, Gunnar Gíslason, Gestur Jóhannesson, Sigfús and Margrét Benedictsson, Jón Kjærnested, Þorsteinn Borgfjörð, and Jón Eldon.

1935, Guttormur Guttormsson of Riverton, Manitoba.

After the turn of the century, the output was still huge, and the Western Icelandic literature maintained its own authentic, distinctive voice. Guttormur J. Guttormsson was the only great poet born in North America writing in classical Icelandic. His poetry is various in style and content. The classic "Sandy Bar" is a magnificent tribute to the early pioneers, acknowledging their perils and achievement in apocalyptic metaphors, but in other poems he

displays satirical wit, humour and disillusionment with modern society. He also wrote interesting symbolical plays. Þorsteinn Þ. Þorsteinsson was an able poet and skilled storyteller, as well as the historian of the emigration. The short stories of Guðrún Helga Finnsdóttir are not very sophisticated in the narrative style, but her wisdom and integrity is perhaps deeper than of any other author of her generation. Her husband was Gísli Jónsson, a fine poet, brother of Einar Páll Jónsson. Jóhannes P. Pálsson was a medical doctor, but in his leisure time he wrote short stories and plays.

Little by little, English became the literary language, which meant that there were new problems to face. Laura Goodman Salverson was the pioneer in writing in English, writing novels which to some extent were a realistic description of the emigration, but fading out into romanticizing the glorious Icelandic heritage. Especially in *The Confessions of an Immigrant's Daughter* she is able to criticise Canadian culture in terms of her own, inherited Icelandic cultural values. Her achievement is great, because she rejected the traditions inherent in the Icelandic language in order to gain ground in the English speaking world.

It was of course inevitable that the language would fade as a literary vehicle. It was beaten out of the children in school, and appears only as a traumatic experience in modern literature. The grandmothers told their children tales and stories. The men continued for decades to tell stories in Icelandic, but one day they realized they were speaking English.

But, they were still telling stories. This storytelling, as well as the multi-faceted experience of their ancestors, is echoing in the works of modern authors of Icelandic descent. Some of them clearly reveal the sheer joy of storytelling in their works. Others deal explicitly with their Icelandic origins. And at the same time, there still exist Icelandic-speaking versemakers writing in the old tradition, composing occasional verse, polemic poems and odes to Iceland, longing for a country they have never seen.

Western Icelandic Drama

Lee Brandson

From the early days of Icelandic settlement in North America through to the second world war, most members of Icelandic communities were involved with amateur drama productions in some capacity. A few wrote or translated plays, many more acted or worked in the background, and virtually everyone else came to watch the productions. The small Icelandic community of Shoal Lake south of Lundar had, for a time, eight active drama societies operating at once. It was not uncommon for a play to run three or four nights in a large hall, and amateur groups from at least Geysir, Gimli, Winnipeg and Wynard took plays on tour through Manitoba, Saskatchewan and North Dakota.

Audiences did not always accept a passive role in these performances. In a play about outlaws, living as best they can in the barren wastes of interior Iceland, the heroine throws her infant child to its death in a waterfall. She explains that she has been cornered by a vigilante group, and fears that the child would suffer a far worse fate at their hands. An outraged reply comes from the audience: I don't care. This is a disgraceful deed.

In the earliest years, plays were performed either out of doors or in the largest log house or barn that was available. In 1883 and 1884 the settlers at Icelandic River (now Riverton) performed in a one room 18 by 24 foot log cabin; the largest home in the settlement. A lucky few got chairs close to the actors, while others learned the true meaning of standing room only as the entire community packed shoulder-to-shoulder into the tiny building.

Many prominent writers tried their hands as playwrights, beginning with none less than Stephan G. Stephansson. He was asked to write a play for the July 4th celebration in Gardar, North Dakota in 1881. He did not accept the task with great enthusiasm:

Stephan and Helga Stephansson.
Photo courtesy *The Icelandic Canadian*.

They demanded that I put together a play. I tried to weasel out of it, but it was no good. I was trapped. I worked [on the farm] every day, but there was plenty of moonlight by night; I lay on the hillside above my cabin every evening and scribbled this rubbish down very quickly, so that it could be learned and rehearsed in time. I was awake the entire night before the performance, all the next day, and the night after. The next day I went to work, and towards evening I fell asleep on the horse-drawn mower. I fell to the ground, but without getting hurt.

His telling of this tale does not quite match the record. His play, this rubbish, was very popular, and circulated

Scald 1 cup of milk. Add to 2½ pounds chopped liver, 1 tablespoon salt, ½ teaspoon freshly ground pepper, 1 pound chopped kidney suet, 1 cup oatmeal and 2½ cups whole wheat flour. Stir thoroughly. Make cotton bags about 4 inches by 8 inches. Wet bags in water, and fill, leaving enough room to sew them closed. Boil for two hours (prick holes in the bag from time to time). Cool, slice and serve either cold or lightly fried.

widely through the Icelandic settlements, to be read and sometimes performed. He also couldn't have objected quite so strongly to the writing of plays, because his papers in the National Archives of Iceland include not only this play in manuscript, but fragments of three other plays as well, and yet another short play was published in an anthology of his work.

No Western Icelandic playwright was more productive than the school-teacher and novelist Jóhann Magnús Bjarnason. He is known to have written at least nineteen full-length plays, and co-wrote at least one more. Most, perhaps all, of these plays were written for his students at the Geysir school to perform. None were published and no manuscripts have been found.

Perhaps the best of the Western Icelandic playwrights was Guttomur J. Guttormsson. He wrote sixteen short plays, generally of very good quality, but only two of his earlier plays were ever performed. His later plays he described as reading plays, most of which would have been difficult or impossible to stage. For example, the character roster of one play includes a variety of body parts and such intangibles as intelligence, feeling and wealth. In another, the players are a child's dirty fingerprints on a wall. Even his more realistic plays would have taxed the most imaginative set crew, such as one play whose characters are insects, and another which takes place in waist-deep snow with a guest appearance by three timber wolves.

Guttormur's only real competition as the foremost Western Icelandic playwright comes from Jóhannes P. Pálsson. He apparently began as a high-school student by co-writing a play with his teacher, Jóhann Magnús Bjarnason. He then co-wrote at least two short plays for an amateur drama group at university in 1909, and continued to write another fifteen one-act plays over the next 50 years. Like Guttormsson, he only had his earliest plays performed. His later plays were well-written and original, but generally far too abstract and symbolic to be easily produced.

Jakob Jónsson deserves honourable mention for two fine plays he wrote for the Wynyard drama society during his five year tenure as Unitarian minister there. He then returned to Iceland, where he studied theatre at the university and became one of the most prominent dramatists in the country.

In all, Western Icelanders are known to have written at least 123 plays, although we only have titles and dates for most of them. Few were published and fewer manuscripts have been found. They also translated at least another 60 plays into Icelandic. Records of translations are extremely poor, and the real number is probably two or three times that high. We can't even guess how many plays were performed – probably thousands.

Western Icelandic dramatic activity reached its peak in the 1920s and early 1930s. This period saw many groups take their plays on tour, and two Icelandic drama competitions were held in Winnipeg in 1927 and 1928 with entries from as far away as Wynyard, Saskatchewan. An Icelandic entry won the *Free Press* shield at the Manitoba Dramatic Festival in 1932. The depression took the wind from the sails of the movement, and the ship was sunk by the Second World War. Few drama societies re-formed after the war, and the last Icelandic language production was held in Geysir in 1951.

The tradition of drama among Western Icelanders has continued, to some extent, through the following decades. A few of the drama societies survived but changed their focus to producing plays in English, including translations from Icelandic. Other drama societies have been formed, such as the New Iceland Drama Society (a student group from the University of Manitoba) that staged some ambitious translations of Icelandic plays at the Icelandic Festival in Gimli and elsewhere during the early and mid 1970s. We also still have our playwrights. David Arnason and W.D. Valgardson have each written both plays and screenplays in recent years. And, of course, these works don't get published. Let us hope that they are more careful with their manuscripts than their predecessors were.

Sources for the Icelandic Canadian Genealogist

Sigrid Johnson

"There was a man called Ketill Flat-Nose, who was the son of Björn Buna. Ketill was a powerful and well-born lord in Norway; he lived in Romsdale, in Romsdale Province, which lies between Sunnmore and Nordmore.

"Ketill Flat-Nose was married to Ingveldur, the daughter of Ketill Weaher, a man of great distinction. They had five children. Their sons were Björn the Easterner and Helgi Bjólan. One daughter was called Þórunn Hyrna; she was the wife of Helgi the Lean. The second daughter was called Unnur the Deep-Minded; she was the wife of Ólafur the White. The third daughter was called Jórunn Wisdom-Slope." (From *Laxdæla Saga*, Chapter 11.)

Genealogy is the third most popular hobby in North America. Throughout their history, the people of Iceland have maintained excellent genealogical records. Their centuries old interest in family record-keeping has been fortunate for the people of Icelandic origin in Canada who have taken up the popular pastime of searching for their roots.

The majority of today's Icelandic Canadian researchers are fourth and fifth generation Canadians. Before they can establish links with the generation that emigrated from Iceland and eventually trace their family's history back to saga times, these researchers must first acquire the details of their family's history in North America. To do this they must begin their research within the family itself. Interviews should be conducted with parents, grandparents, aunts, uncles and cousins in order to obtain as much first-hand information as possible about their ancestors. Not only will this provide them with the basic information which will eventually assist them in extending their pedi-

grees back to Iceland, but it will also provide them with a glimpse into the everyday lives of past generations.

A vast amount of information important to the Icelandic Canadian researcher is contained within the numerous publications of the Icelanders in North America. The generation that emigrated from Iceland brought with it a centuries-old literary tradition which was continued in the new land with the publication of books, periodicals and newspapers describing the historical evolution of Icelandic culture in North America and documenting the lives of the individuals who played a part in this evolution.

For the genealogical researcher, the most valuable of these publications are those which contain biographies of the Icelanders in North America. Such biographical sketches not only contain basic information about a particular individual such as date and place of birth, names of parents, spouse(s), and children, places of residence, and date and place of death, but also often contain information about ancestors and places of origin in Iceland, which enable researchers to establish links with the last generaton of their forefathers to live in Iceland. Among the most useful of these publications are: Thorleifur Jackson's three monographs: *Brot af landnámssögu Nýja Íslands* (Winnipeg: Columbia Press, 1919), *Frá austri til vesturs* (Winnipeg: Columbia Press, 1921), and *Framhald á landnámssögu Nýja Íslands* (Winnipeg: Columbia Press, 1923); Þorsteinn þ. Þorsteinsson and Tryggvi J. Oleson's *Saga Íslendinga í vesturheimi* 5 vols. (Reykjavík: Menningarsjóður; Winnipeg: Þjóðræknisfélag Íslendinga í vesturheimi, 1940–1953); Thorstina Jackson's *Saga Íslendinga í Norður Dakota*

LUMMUR

Lummur are ordinary pancakes.

To make:
Mix 1 cup flour, 2 teaspoons baking powder, two tablespoons sugar and a pinch of salt. Then, in another bowl, mix 1 egg, 1 cup of milk, 2 tablespoons melted butter and ½ teaspoon vanilla. Add dry ingredients to wet and stir until mixed but not beaten. Allow to stand about 45 minutes. Fry on griddle until bubbles appear and pancake looks lacy (two or three minutes). Turn over and fry for about another minute. Serve as you would ordinary pancakes (syrup, sugar, jelly).

(Winnipeg: The City Printing & Publishing Co., 1926); Benjamín Kristjánsson's *Vestur íslenzkav æviskrár* 5 vols. (Akureyri: Bókaforlag Odds Björnssonar, 1961–1985); *Minningarrit íslenzkra hermanna 1914–1918* (Winnipeg: Félagið Jón Sigurðsson I.O.D.E., 1929); and *Veterans of Icelandic descent, World War II* (Winnipeg: Jón Sigurðsson Chapter I.O.D.E., 1990).

Also valuable for the biographical information contained therein is the periodical *Almanak Ólafs S. Thorgeirssonar* vols. 1–60 (Winnipeg: Ólafur S. Thorgeirsson, 1895–1954). Each volume of the *Almanak* highlighted a different North American Icelandic settlement providing an historical overview of the area and biographical sketches of its' pioneer settlers. As well, each volume of the *Almanak* contained a section of death notices, college graduations and official appointments of North American Icelanders. When *Almanak* ceased publication in 1954 this section was continued in *Tímarit Þjóðræknisfélags Íslendinga* vols. 1–50 (Winnipeg: Þjóðræknisfélag Íslendinga í vesturheimi, 1919–1969) until, it too, ceased publication in 1969.

Newspapers are another important printed source for the Icelandic Canadian genealogist, particularly for the biographical information contained in the obituary sections. These newspapers have been published continuously from the time Icelanders first came to Canada up until the present day. The first newspaper was *Nýi Þjóðólfur,* a handwritten newspaper, issued during the winter of 1876. It was followed by *Framfari* (Lundi: Prentfjelag Nýja Íslands, 1877–1880), *Leifur* (Winnipeg: H. Jónsson, 1883–1886), *Heimskringla* (Winnipeg, 1886–1959), *Lögberg-Heimskringla,* an amalgamation of the previous two newspapers, (Winnipeg, 1959–present).

Also noteworthy are the numerous church periodicals including *Árdís* (Winnipeg: Bandalag lúterska kvenna, 1933–1966), *Sameiningin* (Winnipeg: Hið ev. lút. kirkjufélag Ísl. í vesturheimi, 1886–1964) and *Heimir* (Winnipeg: Hið íslenzka únítaraska kirkjufélag í vesturheimi, 1904–1914) and private newspapers and periodicals such as *The Icelandic Canadian* (Winnipeg, 1942–present). In addition to obituaries, these publications contained notices of important events in the Icelandic communities which often included information of a personal nature pertaining to the individuals involved. Indexes to some of these newspapers and periodicals have been or are in the process of being created. For the most part, however, it is necessary to search through each issue when searching for information on an ancestor or a family, a labour intensive task indeed!

In a category all its own is Júníus H. Kristinsson's *Vesturfaraskrá 1870–1914: A record of emigrants from Iceland to America 1870–1914* (Reykjavík: Sagnfræðistofnun Háskóla Íslands, 1983). To discover whether or not a particular ancestor emigrated to North America this is the source to consult. *Vesturfaraskrá* lists, according to farm or town, all inhabitants who emigrated to North America between 1870 and 1914. The information provided includes the year of departure, age, occupation, port of departure, name of ship and point of destination.

Not to be overlooked when searching for information on ancestors' backgrounds and genealogies are government documents and both general and local histories written on the areas where the Icelandic people settled in North America. These publications provide genealogical information and they enable researchers to place their forefathers in the context of the times in which they lived.

A government report of particular note is Baldwin L. Baldwinson's "Report on the Icelandic settlements in Canada, 1891–92" published in the *Dominion Sessional Papers* (Ottawa: Department of the Interior, 7:1892, 13:1893). These reports cover all the major Icelandic settlements in Canada. Listed are the names of the heads of the families in each settlement together with information on their financial standing. Of particular importance to the genealogist is the information on place of origin in Iceland.

General histories such as Wilhelm Kristjanson's *The Icelandic people in Manitoba* (Winnipeg: Wallingford

Press, 1965, reprinted 1990); Walter J. Lindal's *The Icelanders in Canada* (Ottawa: National Publishers; Winnipeg: Viking Printers, 1967); Walter J. Lindal's *The Saskatchewan Icelanders* (Winnipeg: Columbia Press, 1955); and Thorstína Jackson's *Modern sagas: the story of the Icelanders in North Dakota* (Fargo, N.D.: North Dakota Institute for Regional Studies, 1953) enable researchers to place events in the lives of their ancestors into the context of the history of Icelandic people in North America.

Icelandic Canadian settlements have not been immune to the local history phenomenon. As each settlement has approached the centenary of its establishment it has not been unusual to receive an announcement of a recently published, or just about to be published, local history of the area. Although local histories often contain considerable errors due to the fact they are based more on personal reminiscences than on historical documentation, these publications are extremely valuable to the genealogist. In fact, local histories are probably the first sources a fifth generation Icelandic Canadian researcher should consult.

Manitoba local histories include: *Come into our heritage: centennial history of Argyle* (Baldur: Rural Municipality of Argyle, 1981); *Patience, pride and progress* (Eddystone: Eddystone and District Historical Soceity, 1983); *Faith and fortitude: a history of the Geysir district, 1880's–1980's* (Arborg: Geysir Historical Society, 1983); Ingibjorg S. McKillop's *Mikley: the magnificent island: treasure of memories: Hecla Island, 1876–1976* (S.1.: I.S. McKillop, 1979); *A century unfolds: history of Arborg and district, 1889–1987* (Arborg: Arborg Historical Society, 1987); *Taming a wilderness: a history of Ashern and district* (Ashern: Ashern Historical Society, 1976); *Gimli saga: the history of*

A.S. Bardal Funeral Home, Gimli.

A farmer takes a break from stooking.

Gimli, Manitoba (Gimli: Women's Institute, 1974); *Along the crocus trail* (Langruth: Langruth Historical Society, 1984); *Wagons to wings: history of Lundar and district, 1872–1980* (Lundar: The Society, 1980); Steinn O. Thompson's *Riverton and the Icelandic River settlement* (Riverton: T. Thompson, 1976); Nelson Gerrard's *Icelandic River saga* (Arborg: Saga Publications, 1985); *When the west was bourne: a history of Westbourne and district, 1860–1985* (Westbourne: Westbourne-Longbourne History, 1985); and Geirfinnur Peterson's *History of the Icelandic settlements at the Narrows, Manitoba* (Winnipeg: Lögberg-Heimskringla, 1970).

Saskatchewan and Alberta local histories useful to the Icelandic Canadian genealogical researcher are: *Reflections by the Quills* (Wynyard: Quill Historical Society, 1981); *From prairie trails to the Yellowhead* (Winnipeg: Inter-Collegiate Press, 1984); *Along the Burnt Lake Trail* (Red Deer: Burnt Lake History Society, 1977) and *Grub-axe to grain* (Calgary: D.W. Friesen & Sons, 1973).

Just as a strong literary tradition fostered a proliferation of publications among the Icelanders in North America, these publications in turn led to the establishment of libraries to house the publications. Numerous libraries across North America contain collections of Icelandic publications. From a genealogical standpoint, however, the most significant collection, in terms of the near complete-ness of its holding and its continuing interest in genealogi-cal materials, is The Icelandic Collection, located in the Elizabeth Dafoe Library at the University of Manitoba. Icelandic Canadian genealogical researchers can therefore consider themselves doubly fortunate on finding that much of the work of tracing their family tree in North America has already been completed for them and is included in the aforecited publications, and on finding that their forefathers had the forethought to establish libraries, such as the University of Manitoba's Icelandic Collection, to house these works for future generations.

Learning the Icelandic Language

Sigrid Johnson

There are as many ways to learn the Icelandic language as there are needs or reasons to do so. Undoubtedly, the best way to learn Icelandic is by travelling to Iceland and enrolling in one of the many excellent programs available to foreign students. Program offerings include: the University of Iceland's two-year course in Icelandic for Foreign Students; a course of study provided by the Reykjavík Municipal Centre for Adult Education (Námsflokkar Reykjavíkur) courses offered by private schools, most notably Mímir; and a summer course held by the University of Iceland and the Sigurður Nordal Institute.

Not everyone wants to or can afford to travel to Iceland to study, so fortunately there are alternatives depending upon one's needs or reasons for wanting to learn Icelandic. Most chapters of the Icelandic National League of North America have at one time or another sponsored courses in conversational Icelandic. The University of Manitoba, through the Department of Icelandic Language and Literature, offers a program of studies leading to degrees at both the Bachelor's and Master's levels. For those living in areas where organized courses are unavailable or for those who are unable to fit organized courses into already hectic schedules, commercial offerings, such as the Linguaphone course on record or cassette, provide a solution.

A large plus for the Linguaphone course is that in addition to its regular course book and exercises, it also provides students with a copy of Stefán Einarsson's *Icelandic: Grammar, Texts, Glossary* first published in Baltimore by The Johns Hopkins University Press in 1949, and unequaled by any Icelandic grammar textbook published to the present day. Not only does the grammar textbook provide the student with a comprehensive treat-

ment of all major aspects of modern Icelandic, it does so without requiring the student to have a considerable background in language theory. It is an important back-up to the Linguaphone material, supplying answers to most problems a student, beginner or advanced, is likely to encounter. Other grammar textbooks worth considering include Jón Friðjónsson's *A Course in Modern Icelandic: Texts, Vocabulary, Grammar Exercises, Translations* (Reykjavík: Tímaritið Skáð, 1978); Einar Pálsson's *Icelandic in Easy Stages,* No's. 1 and 2, (Reykjavík: Mímir, 1975-1977); and Ásta Svavarsdóttir and Margrét Jónsdóttir's *Íslenska fyrir útlendinga: kennslubók í málfræði* (Reykjavík: Málvísindastofnun Háskóla Íslands, 1988), which is accompanied by Ásta Svavarsdóttir's exercises, *Æfingar: með enskum glósum og leiðréttingalyklum* (Reykjavík: Málvísindastofnun Háskóla Íslands, 1989). Also useful to the student of Icelandic are Ari Páll Kristinsson's *Pronunciation of Modern Icelandic: a brief course for foreign students* (Reykjavík: Málvísindastofnun Háskóla Íslands, 1988), along with its accompanying cassette, and P.J.T. Glendinning's *Teach Yourself Icelandic* (London: The English Universities Press, 1969).

It has been said that "Dictionaries are as vital to the language learner as cans of beans to the long distance hiker, and come in as many varieties."[1] Dictionaries – Icelandic, Icelandic-English, English-Icelandic – which no student of the Icelandic language should be without include: Árni Böðvarsson's Icelandic dictionary, *Íslensk orðabók handa skólum og almenningi* 2nd. ed. (Reykjavík: Menningarsjóður, 1983); Ásgeir Blöndal Magnússon's Icelandic etymological dictionary, *Íslensk orðsifjabók* (Reykjavík: Orðabók Háskólans, 1989); the Icelandic dictionary of synonyms and antonyms edited by

Programs of study:
Icelandic for Foreign Students,
Háskóli Íslands við Suðurgötu,
Reykjavík 101, Iceland

Department of Icelandic Language & Literature,
University of Manitoba,
Winnipeg, MB
R3T 2N2, Canada

Sigurður Nordal Institute,
P.O. Box 1220,
Reykjavík 121, Iceland

Námsflokkar Reykjavikur,
Fríkirkjuvegi 1,
Reykjavík 101, Iceland

Mímir málaskóli,
Ánanaustum 15,
Reykjavík 101, Iceland

Bookstore:
Bókabúð Máls og menningar,
Laugavegi 18,
Reykjavík 101, Iceland

DAVID ARNASON

To grow up in Gimli in the early forties was to be bathed in the Icelandic language. I never learned to speak it, because my parents were determined that I would not sound like an immigrant, and so they did not speak it at home. Nevertheless, it was always there, a sort of background hum like voices in another room. I spent a lot of time on my grandparents' farm, and so I learned to get around in it, which is to say that I learned whole blocks of sound that told me what the moods and feelings and intentions that surrounded me were. And I learned large configurations of vowels and consonants that told when it was time to fetch the cows, or shovel the barn or go for lunch. In a real sense, I drifted with the conversation – picking up chunks of meaning here and there, so I knew what the topic was, what had happened to whom, how it all ended. I could even respond in long sentences, provided I was asked the right questions. But I didn't know the words. I didn't know where one word ended and the other began. I could speak whole phrases or sentences, carry on a conversation about work and weather for minutes at a time, but I suppose I only knew the whole meaning of what I said and none of its parts.

It didn't bother me though. My friends didn't speak Icelandic any better than I did. We assumed that it was a language spoken only by adults, and used particularly for secrets or for things we weren't supposed to know about, and I, at least, believed that I would naturally speak it when I grew older. All I had to do was wait. Of course that didn't happen, but I've lost none of my love for the mystical language that drifts at the edges of my comprehension. When I hear Icelandic spoken, I am warmed. I feel an instant kinship with the speakers, though I may or may not know what they are talking about. There are smells that conjure with amazing force our memories of childhood. For me, Icelandic is like that. A phrase caught in passing can be a hayfield in July, a storm on Lake Winnipeg, or the arms of my grandmother. The lilting singsong rhythms of that ancient langage are the beat my heart moves to when I am happy.

—David Arnason

Svavar Sigmundsson, *Íslensk samheitaorðabók* (Reykjavík: Styrktarsjóður Þórbergs Þóðarsonar, 1985); Icelandic-English dictionaries such as Richard Cleasby's and Guðbrandur Vig-fússon's *An Icelandic-English Dictionary* 2nd. ed. (Oxford: Clarendon Press, 1957), Arngrímur Sigurðsson's *Íslensk-Ensk orðabók = Concise Icelandic-English Dictionary* edited by Sverrir Hólmarsson, Christopher Sanders and John Tucker (Reykjavík: Iðunn, 1989); English-Icelandic dictionaires including Sigurður Örn Bogason's *Ensk-Íslensk orðabók* (Reykjavík: Ísafold, 1976), Sören Sörenson's *Ensk-Íslensk orðabók með alfræðilegu ívafi* (Reykjavík: Örn og Örlygur, 1984), and Jón Skaptason's *Ensk-Íslensk skólaorðabók* (Reykjavík: Örn og Örlygur, 1986); and depending upon a student's subject interests, specialty dictionaries such as Þórir Einarsson's and Terry G. Lacy's dictionaries of business terms, *Íslensk-Ensk viðskiptaorðabók* (Reykjavík: Örn og Örlygur, 1989)and *Ensk-Íslensk viðskiptaorðabók* (Reykjavík: Örn og Örlygur, 1982), Hálfdan Ómar Hálfdanarson's dictionary of biological terms *Ensk-Íslensk orðaskrá í líffræði* (Reykjavík: Hálfdan O. Hálfdanarson, 1981), and Eiríkur Rögnvaldsson's dictionary which concentrates on rhyme, *Rímorðabók* (Reykjavík: Iðunn, 1989).

Whatever the need or reason to learn Icelandic, with a little investigation a student is sure to discover just the right program of studies, just the right grammar textbook and just the right dictionary.

Most commercial course materials such as those offered by Linguaphone and grammar textbooks can be special-ordered through your local bookstore. Icelandic language dictionaries, on the other hand, are not typically stocked by North American bookstores and are best purchased directly from Iceland.

1. B.S., "From friendly strangers to lifelong companions," in *News From Iceland,* December 1985, p. 14.

The Gimli Waltz

Frank Olson, in conjunction with an excellent translation of the lyrics of the Gimli Waltz, states:

"The Gimli Waltz was introduced and popularized in the early days of the New Iceland colony by the late revered Óli Thorsteinson of Húsavík, Manitoba. The Icelandic lyric was written by the late Jón Jónatanson of Gimli and Winnipeg. It has been played, sung, danced to and cherished with nostalgic fervour by New Icelanders since the turn of the present century."

O'er dreamland's mystic shores, my spirit hovers light
On wings of song it soars, this silent winter night.
Though far afield it fare, it e'er returns to thee.
Light of my love and life's guiding star to me.
   Bliss, heavenly bliss, rock me to rest.
   Kiss, fervently kiss, lips tenderly pressed.
   Sleep, lull me to sleep, in your arms caressed.
   Let me dream of Love's rapturous summertime
                  Sun maiden blest.

So through this wondrous world, we drift in dreams divine,
My right arm round you curled, and left hand clasped in thine.
Thus swirling cheek to cheek, we find eternal grace.
Two hearts as one, beating now as we embrace.
   Soar peacefully, soar; sweet ecstacy!
   Clear, perfectly clear to you and to me.
   Love, Oh perfect love, to our souls revelaed.
   Tra, la, la, la, la, la, la, la, la, la, la;
                  blooms though concealed.

Translated by Frank Olson, born Gimli, June 1, 1898.

A Final Word

We live two lives, our life in the everyday world of duty and responsibility where we are happy or sad in turn, and our life in imagination where the world takes on the shape of our desire. Art is what takes our dreams out of the evanescent moment and gives them a tangible reality. It allows what is private to become public, what exists only in a fleeting present to become re-presented, to take on the shape of a poem, a painting, a play or a photograph. Our bodies are fragile and we die, but art gives our imagination a kind of immortality.

Iceland has no long tradition of visual representation, though the early manuscripts are stunningly illustrated, and there is now a vital artistic community producing paintings and sculptures. We can search in vain for the great historic Icelandic painters. There are none, and the few paintings of Icelanders that exist before the late nineteenth century are imported, the work of foreign artists. The first great painter of Icelandic subjects and ordinary Icelanders was my great-great-grandfather, Arngrímur Gíslason. Among his paintings is a portrait of his father-in-law, Hjörleifur Guttormormsson, painted about 1850. That ancestor remains a presence, even though he is long dead, and he is present because an artist looked at him and imagined an arrangement of paint on canvas.

Literature was the chief art of the Icelanders, and the historic sagas and eddas are Iceland's great gift to the world. The Icelanders who came to Canada continued the tradition. For those settlers, poetry was no arcane art. It was the most natural way of expressing yourself. Almost everyone wrote, and the number who published their works is astonishingly large for a small community. Beyond that, the oral verse tradition of the *kvæðirímur* was alive and well, and many of the settlers were adept at insulting each other in rhyme. The literary tradition has continued unabated into the twentieth century.

A new art form, photography, was just coming into its own as the Icelanders arrived in the new world. Every family had its portrait taken, and together we have a giant archive of our apparently grim and upright ancestors. But there's something of a lie in that representation. Photographs were expensive. They were taken at special occasions when people dressed in their Sunday finest and were posed by professional photographers in arrangements that could never occur in life. Nobody smiles, not because they didn't want to, but because the slow shutter speeds of those old cameras wouldn't capture anything so fleeting as a smile.

Still, even then, the Icelandic community revealed a peculiar sense of play. Not satisfied with the formality of the studio, they moved outside, dressed in costumes, and presented themselves as they wanted to be seen. A photograph of croquet players, who would not be out of place on an upper-class British lawn, seem surreal against the

Photo from the collection of Kristin Kristofferson in the archives of Terry Tergesen.

backdrop of a pioneer farm. In another photograph of the same period, a family has gathered on the banks of Willow Creek for what might have been a typical representation, except that some of the family members are seated in a boat and a pair of young girls, fully clothed, stand up to their waists in water to steady it. The photographer is apparently somewhere in the middle of the creek.

By the 1920s, the camera had become the most democratic of all forms. The cost of photographs had dropped dramatically, and the portrait was giving way to the snapshot. What was surreal in the old photographs was natural in the new, the result of a sense of play and a desire to represent oneself as a creature of imagination, not as a branch of the family tree. Everywhere now, an innocent and playful photographer's eye catches a culture expressing its fantasies. Women dress as men. Men dress as cowboys or as decadent European dandies, complete with monocle. Women in bathing suits dance in the snow. Small children in their parent's clothes give each other a pre-sexual kiss. These are not events that occurred and were merely recorded. The camera itself created the occasion, and the photographs are both more and less realistic than other representation. The backgrounds are no longer photographer's sets, but actual places, yet the events are all pre-imagined. Later, the "snapshot" of things that were "really happening" would become the dominant photographic mode, but for a brief time, between the days of the old style professional photographer and the relentless snapshooter, there was room for a democratic art of representation.

In our research for this book, we came on a startling archive of photographs. Most of them were taken by or arranged by Benneta Benson, a beautiful young woman who was born in 1913 and died tragically in 1933 at the age of twenty. In the five years between fifteen and twenty, she discovered the camera and by the time of her death had become serious enough about it that she was developing her own photographs.

Three beautiful young women dress as gypsies and dance in the snow. Their high-heeled and open shoes are wholly

Photos from the collection of Kristin Kristofferson in the archives of Terry Tergesen.

Photos from the collection of
Kristin Kristofferson in the archives
of Terry Tergesen.

inappropriate. They strike elaborate poses that they must know only from books and magazines. There were no gypsy dancers in Gimli in the 1920s. The central figure gives a high sign to the missing photographer. There is an unmistakable sign of carnival and joy in this photo. The fierce Manitoba winter is ritually tamed.

In another formation, another three young women, their backs to the wall, their legs apart, take on a posture of deliberate eroticism, though their faces are full of innocence. They are costumed as big girls playing little girls pretending to be big girls, a double imposture, a knowing parody. As a kind of contrast, Benneta has two of her friends dress as nuns and hold bibles, their faces somber and pious. Why did they want to represent themselves this way? Or again, Benneta dresses as a bride in white. Her groom is another young woman dressed as a man. The photographs are filled with ritual inversions and play.

In still another photograph, this one taken at the cemetery in Hnausa, two young women casually lean on a gravestone, smiling for the camera. A third in front of the stone, kneels, hands clasped with flowers in apparent prayer. Why this gentle blasphemy, this toying with the idea of death?

Finally, Benneta poses behind an umbrella in an open field. Her sister, the novelist Kristin Benson Kristofferson, who often found herself posed for photographs, told me that the photo was occasioned by an excess of modesty. The photo was taken by a boy whose name has been long forgotten. Benneta was wearing a very short bathing suit, and did not wish him to have a picture of her so undressed. Instead she offered a pose that suggests she is naked behind her umbrella.

Together, these photos suggest a world of imagination and play alongside the daily life of work. The inhabitants of New Iceland took their art seriously. They wrote poetry and plays and novels, and had deep respect for the artist in the community. But the artist was never some special being separate from the rest of the group. They seem to have believed that, given the right opportunity and the right materials, anyone could produce art. Benneta's photographs suggest to me that they were right.

About the Editors

David Arnason is a writer, editor, critic and Professor of Canadian Literature at the University of Manitoba. His books include *The Pagan Wall, The Circus Performers Bar, The Happiest Man in the World,* and, for Turnstone Press, *Skrag, Fifty Stories and a Piece of Advice, Marsh Burning, The Dragon and the Dry Goods Princess* and *If Pigs Could Fly.* He resides in Winnipeg and owns a summer cottage and a full-season studio on Willow Island.

Vincent Arnason resides year-round at his home on Willow Island, and operates a general contracting firm.

Father and son are direct descendants of the original Icelandic settlers. Willow Island is a scenic spit of land on Lake Winnipeg, and the exact spot on which their ancestors landed in 1875.